HOW TO
WRITE
EFFECTIVE
POLICIES AND
PROCEDURES

THE SYSTEM THAT MAKES THE PROCESS OF DEVELOPING POLICIES AND PROCEDURES EASY

KIRSTEN BRUMBY

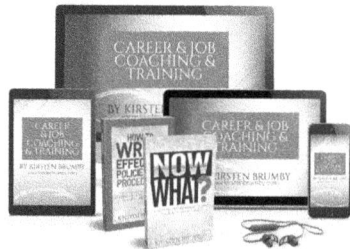

HOW TO
WRITE
EFFECTIVE
POLICIES AND
PROCEDURES

THE SYSTEM THAT MAKES THE PROCESS OF DEVELOPING POLICIES AND PROCEDURES EASY

KIRSTEN BRUMBY

MP

Mind Potential Publishing
by The Potentialist

Author: Kirsten Brumby | www.kirstenbrumby.com
Title: How to Write Effective Policies and Procedures
ISBN Paperback: 978-1-922380-33-3
ISBN Kindle: 978-1-922380-35-7
Category: Business | Reference

A catalogue record for this book is available from the National Library of Australia

Publisher: Mind Potential Publishing
Division of Mind Design Centre Pty Ltd,
PO Box 6094, Maroochydore BC
Queensland, Australia, 4558. International Phone: +61 405 138 567
Australia Phone: 1300 664 544 | www.mindpotentialpublishing.com

Cover design by NGirl Design | www.ngirldesign.com.au

Printed in Australia

DEDICATION

It's hard to dedicate this book to someone. Who in their right mind would want a policy and procedure book dedicated to them? So instead, I dedicate this book to lots of someone's. When the decision was made that someone needs to, or someone should, write those pesky policies and procedures, it was you that it fell to.

So, to all those someone's – all the many people I have helped develop and write their policies and procedures, thank you. It is you that helped form the process and tools you find inside, and so it is to you I dedicate this book.

I also dedicate this book to you, my reader, because I know the job you have ahead of you, and I appreciate the position you are in. Here's the thing though, if you're reading this book and you don't actually have to develop or maintain policies and procedures, then you might need to re-examine the way you like to spend your spare time! ☺

CONTENTS

WHAT OTHERS HAVE TO SAY...

"I loved this book. Simple to read, conversational style and enjoyable despite the dry topic. An easy to read book to guide good policy writing and formulation of sound procedures. Well done Kirsten!"

Yvonne Porter,
Manager, Community and Social Services Sector

—— ◊ —— ◊ —— ◊ ——

"Choose your own adventure! Though I've written many policies and procedures for small to medium size organisations, I was struggling to rewrite a particularly tricky set of procedures and realised I needed to go back to basics or follow a recipe. After recently reading "What now?", imagine my delight to discover that Kirsten had also written a book about how to write effective policies and procedures.

As you'd expect, this recipe for the perfect set of policies and procedures is logically ordered, has relatable and relevant case studies and can be adjusted to suit. But, more than that, Kirsten's writing style is truly engaging. By breaking with convention, using emphasis and writing in a conversational way, Kirsten is somehow there in the room telling the stories, explaining the how, who, why and why not. It's reassuring, which I know is exactly the feeling to have when you're about to embark on a monumental task like writing policies and procedures!

As an added bonus, the templates are ready to download and adapt. I now have the confidence to get this job done!"

KL,
Project Officer, State Government

"This book is a fabulous resource for any organisation. Having faced the mammoth task of starting from scratch and then implementing this particular system for our organisational Policies and Procedures, I can attest to the quality and usability of the output. And now I have the perfect resource to enable me to stay on track with creating, updating, reviewing and maintaining these in my organisation. Easy to read and fabulous examples of how good policies and procedures can benefit an organisation, its employees and customers. Perfect!!"

Stephanie Cusack,
CFO, Community and Social Services Sector

Whether it's your first time or you are an old hand, this is a great read for anyone faced with the daunting task of writing or developing policy and procedures. Kirsten delivers a simple yet comprehensive guide to writing policy and procedures. Case studies and her straight forward instructions, make this guide both practical and easy to follow.

What I loved about this book was the human focus throughout, with great advice on how to get your people to engage with the development and use of your policy and procedures. After all, if nobody reads or understands your policy and procedure what was the point of all that hard work writing them?"

Tracey Cremming,
Manager, State Government

INTRODUCTION

I often admit being a bit boring because I'm enthusiastic about policies and procedures. In reality I am a self-confessed and proud pragmatist when it comes to policy and procedure – somebody has to do them, right?

Now, I wouldn't go so far as to say I'm a tragic or start preaching about policies and procedures being a panacea to every problem – that they can 'fix' your organization and can make all things better. I can't say that, because it's simply not true. What I can say is that where policies and procedures are concerned, I've become a realist. Let me tell you how I got there.

For a period of time I consulted with an organization to enhance the operations of their busy office. I looked at all facets of their administration and clerical duties, and part of my remit was to evaluate and improve the bookkeeping and accounts area. There were existing staff members in the administration and customer service roles, so I was able to take a hands-off reviewing role for these activities. However, at the start of the consulting assignment, I agreed to take on the duties of the bookkeeper while reviewing the tasks, as there had been an unexpected vacancy in the job at the same time I came on board.

No worries I thought, I've kind-of done this before, it's not that hard, and it will give me a chance to review things from a hands-on position, while a new person is recruited into the role. You might already be smarter than I was at the time and have guessed

Happiness is a hot cup of tea and a handful of policies and procedures.

that it was harder than I thought it would be, and you'd be right. Let me just say, I am not good at bookkeeping. Possibly that is an understatement, it is definitely a particular set of skills needing some affinity for it, and numbers are just not my forte. I find them frustrating and my brain just doesn't seem to make sense of what has to be done with them.

For each task, I would painstakingly and laboriously figure out what I had to do – print this report, take that figure from the report and put it in this field in the accounting software. Then run a different report and take this amount and write it on a form to send to the Taxation Office. I would momentarily be proud I had figured it out, and then move straight onto the next thing. Because I was just working things out to get the job done, I never really understood what I was doing. And because this was a temporary job for me, I didn't want to invest the time and energy into getting a deeper understanding of it. So, when the next week (or month) rolled around and I had to do the same task, I had to again figure it all out from scratch! I got increasingly frustrated as I went through the same processes over and over, but the time taken for each task was not getting any shorter. I became miserable as each time I did this, my incompetence and inability to understand the tasks or remember them, glared at me. I also felt guilty as I was charging an hourly rate for this work and didn't feel as if I was earning my money or providing the organization with value from my being there.

It was on one particularly frustrating day, trying many different ways of achieving a task, when I happened to scrawl on a piece of paper a few notes while working out an especially complicated sequence of steps. I shoved the notes in the desk drawer in my rush to leave the office at the end of the day.

The next time I had to do this particular task I groaned inwardly at the thought, made myself a cup of tea for fortitude and sat down at the computer. As I began, it all came back in a rush to me – not the steps I needed to take, for those I had no idea, but feeling stupid and frustrated that I couldn't remember how to do it easily. And then, probably fueled by my despair, I suddenly remembered that I had written notes, and they may have survived in the drawer. I scrabbled through the drawer until I found the piece of paper and with a burst of adrenaline, completed the task in record time, using the notes I had made previously.

I sat back in my chair incredulous that what had taken me a few hours a month ago, had just taken me less time than it took for my tea to cool down to drinking temperature. Not only was the feeling of relief huge, but I felt smart because I'd done the job quickly and easily because I'd used my initiative to find the notes and reuse them. It was a positive experience that set up the rest of my day.

In fact, it set up the rest of my time there. I'll admit, I went a bit crazy and documented everything I did in that bookkeeping role, writing little mini-procedures and adding to them or tweaking them as I went. The more bookkeeping tasks I had a procedure for, the faster I became at undertaking those tasks, freeing me up to do the process review work I was originally brought in to do. I also made significantly less errors, again saving time and avoiding those embarrassing letters from the Taxation Officer pointing out my mistakes!

Most surprisingly, I *felt* great. I now looked forward to going into work at this assignment, I no longer felt stupid and although the bookkeeping tasks were still not fun for me, they were no longer the ordeal they had been.

As I worked through the process review of all the operations for the organization, my new-found freedom from bookkeeping through procedures, stuck with me and I began to see opportunities to develop other procedures across the organization as well. This was a huge success, as they had a number of part-time staff whose duties overlapped.

The staff were experiencing frustration that things weren't done the same way by different people, or someone would start something and then someone else would need to finish it, but not know where it was up to. Handing over customer service matters between staff was a nightmare and was resulting in poor customer satisfaction.

Providing a procedure for who did what, how and when, for a number of tasks split across staff members proved a life-saver for them. I had the opportunity to see the same outcomes I had experienced with the bookkeeping play out with other areas and staff, across operations. The staff raved to their boss (my client) about how amazing it was now that they had these procedures in place. The client commented to me how happy he was, now that his staff were so much happier, and that he'd had feedback from customers saying they were much happier with the service they were receiving, with time to resolve matters now not being reliant on a staff member's work days in the office.

And there was icing on this particular cake. When it was time to finish up my contract with them, I helped to recruit a bookkeeper and they came on board while I was still there in order to handover the bookkeeping duties. And I bet you've guessed again – handover was an absolute cinch. I used the procedures for handover, and armed with these, the new bookkeeper was productive immediately. And although they wouldn't have experienced anywhere near the angst I did when I first started (as they knew what they were doing!), they had very little stress in working out how, what and when things were done in this organization.

"It's true.
A good set of policies and procedures makes me happy.
They can make you happy too."

So, that's how I began my journey to become a policy and procedure pragmatist – writing practical instructions to solve problems that made me look better than I really was (as a bookkeeper anyway). But while I wrote procedures which helped the organization and individuals working there, don't be fooled into thinking that the procedures I wrote back then were *good*. They certainly would not pass muster now – in fact, they wouldn't even get close. I've since learned, and put into practice many times,

► how to write effective policies and procedures

► and how not to write them too

► what to definitely put in

► and what not to put in, and

► even why to write them, or

► why not to write them at all

Fittingly, writing policies and procedures, or documenting processes, is just a process that I've developed which can be used by you to develop your own. A process to simplify what looks like a complicated mess, and an enormous effort, into manageable tasks, using an understandable structure that you can replicate many times over.

Let's get going…

Kirsten Brumby

CHAPTER 1
Short Term Pain Versus Long Term Gain

As I learned during my first foray into writing policies and procedures, there are some really good reasons to write them. I was fortunate to see the positive outcomes for that organization in terms of improved customer and staff satisfaction, improved service and time efficiencies. I count myself fortunate that I was directly and positively impacted as my personal

You'll wish you had policies and procedures the moment you need them.

situation in that assignment improved markedly due to their introduction. It turned what could have been a monumental failure in my consulting career into a rather startling success.

If someone had told me at the start of that assignment that they knew a way to make me happier in my role, to feel less stupid and incompetent, and be able to improve my efficiency and effectiveness significantly – I probably would have been skeptical, but I would have also jumped at the opportunity, even if it was going to cost me time in the short term.

If we are honest with each other, the only reason you are reading this book is that you either

1. Know you need to write policies and procedures and perhaps have even been putting that off or dreading it because you don't know where to start… or

2. You have been given the responsibility to write them for someone else in your organization (probably because no-one else put their hand up or wanted to).

In both cases, you probably don't need to spend any time justifying why they're a good thing – you just need to get them done. Not many people write them by choice, and even less of us write them for fun.

However, you will make the task far more palatable when you reframe your thinking about policies and procedures and understand why the short-term pain will be well and truly worth the long-term gain.

How you *benefit* from policies and procedures

It's worthwhile spending time exploring the benefits of having policies and procedures in place in an organization, not to justify you doing them or give you a reason to do them. I'm not trying to convince you that you *should* have them, this is simply to make you feel better about having to do them.

1. **Consistency is key.** Documenting rules and ways to do things within an organization and then actually using them, helps to create a consistent product or service no matter the person doing the work to create the product or deliver the service. It won't matter about the location of where the product is being

made or service is being delivered, or many other variables, the results will be consistent. In the organization of my earlier consulting engagement, documenting "the way things are done around here" was key in improving customer service due to the part-time nature of staff. All team members were able to handover customer matters seamlessly to be dealt with by another staff member on the next shift.

Possibly the most famous example of this in practice is McDonalds fast food restaurants, where their strictly adhered to policies and procedures across the whole of the organization and operations – suppliers, building design, recruitment and training, and food preparation – allows for a nearly identical food experience across the world. While you probably don't want to go to that crazy level, imagine just a measure of this consistency in *your* world, *your* work, the reason *you* are developing your policies and procedures. Fabulous!

2. **Time is money.** With policies and procedures in place and being utilized, the potential to save time, money and effort is huge. I wasn't exaggerating earlier when I said that once I had a procedure I could refer to, a task that had taken me hours took less time than a cup of tea cooling to drinkable temperature. And in this case the cost saving to the organization was immediately and easily reconcilable. I was being paid an hourly rate and I cut down substantially the hours dedicated to these tasks. Not to mention the onboarding cost for the new bookkeeper was significantly reduced as they were immediately productive, and required very little of my time, or theirs, for handover.

3. **Happiness is… a little support.** A little less tangible in my example, was the happiness of people undertaking the work. My client, unsolicited by me, gave me that exact feedback. The staff were reporting that they were happier in their jobs

because of the procedures. And the customers also reported they were 'happier' with their service now. There is no doubt that I felt happier in my role, I felt competent and that I was getting the job done, done well and done efficiently, for my client. I didn't think about it in these terms at the time, but this is certainly something I've seen many times since in my different policy and procedure projects.

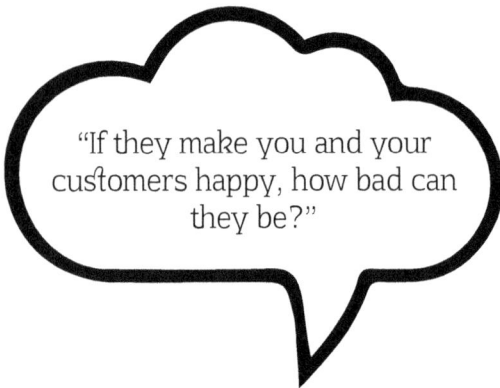

> "If they make you and your customers happy, how bad can they be?"

I wouldn't blame you for being a little skeptical of this one, so let me explain *why* I think increased happiness can happen. People like to feel supported in their work. Support can obviously take many forms in the workplace, such as mentoring or coaching and supervision. Policies and procedures can not only support people, but also make them *feel* supported. It can be a great comfort to know that you are doing the right thing, at the right time, in the right way. And policies and procedures can support you by laying out clearly what is 'right.'

Although we are focusing on why policies and procedures are so great, it would be remiss of me not to point out that badly written or poorly implemented policies and procedures can have the opposite effect on people and have other drawbacks as well. Unfortunately, poorly implemented policies and procedures are quite common, which is why they have such a bad reputation generally. Badly written or poorly implemented policies and procedures can stifle creativity and initiative and cause unnecessary frustration and stress for staff and customers.

Why you *Need* policies and procedures

In the case of my client, you could have argued successfully that policies and procedures were something that this organization didn't *really* need. They're not usually an essential part of core business, so this is true for some organizations. However, many organizations don't *realize* they need them, until they *actually* need them. And when an organization finds itself in a position where they *need* policies and procedures, they usually really, *really* need them. This can happen for a number of reasons:

1. Compliance with governmental laws or regulations. If you think reading and adhering to organizational policies is hard, try reading and adhering to an Act of legislation. You *need* policies and procedures within your organization when there is a requirement for your employees (and hence your organization) to be compliant, for example, with discrimination or workplace health and safety laws and regulations. Complicated legislation and regulations can be simplified and translated into easy to follow policies and procedures for an organization and employees to follow while ensuring organizational compliance.

2. The organization actively seeks, or is required to seek, an accreditation or a qualification that requires them to have certain policies and procedures. Even if funding is sought from some authorities, it may be a requirement that certain policies and procedures are in place. For example, I was engaged to develop a suite of housing policies and procedures that covered property and tenant management and maintenance. The community services organization I worked with sought accreditation to provide government housing for welfare recipients and these were a prerequisite to achieving the accreditation.

Why you *Want* policies and procedures

The Bye-bye Board's story

I was brought in as a consultant to work with an organization when a very serious employee grievance was lodged by a large number of the staff against one of their senior employees. They had no policy or procedure in place for dealing with grievances, and because there was no internal process for dealing with this matter, the staff lodged the grievance with the primary funding body for the organization. The threat of funding being cut-off was imminent.

I was brought in by the board, at considerable cost to the organization, to investigate and work through the grievance. Client services, management and employees all suffered for three months while the grievance was investigated, and outcomes reported and delivered. It also caused a mass resignation from the board that was in place at the time, and a huge upheaval within the organization.

The original board members who found themselves in the position where there was no policy and procedure, desperately wished that they had a policy to guide them and/or a procedure to follow. Unfortunately, their position was not tenable because there was not, and the grievance quickly escalated to the point where they felt they had to resign. The new board, and staff, learning from this experience, actively *wanted* to introduce policies and procedures.

This organization had *no* policies and procedures at all in place, so one of the recommendations from my review of the grievance was to set up a full suite across all functional areas of the organization. Following the grievance investigation, I was engaged to develop these, which I did in conjunction with staff and the board.

Fast forward two years, and another significant staff grievance arose. Instead of going to the funding body, the correct procedure was followed by staff, and the grievance was received by the (new) board. It was a simple matter of following the process through agreed policies and procedures, which had clear rules for the investigation and resolution of staff grievances. For the board and staff members involved, the process took minimal time and although the issue itself was stressful for those involved, the process did not add to their distress. There was no upheaval for any part of the organization and customer service was not affected.

Having been brought in again to investigate the grievance, I was able to swiftly and efficiently look into it according to their procedure, provide a report and recommendations, and the board was able to effectively and efficiently resolve it without involving the funding body, or any other non-involved staff.

Still need convincing?

There is no doubt that putting policies and procedures in place will cause short-term pain as they need focus, time and effort to put them in place.

I'm not here to convince you to develop policies and procedures, I am neither a fervent fan, nor a huge hater – you will recall I am a policy and procedure pragmatist. Some organizations need them, some want them, and they are of great benefit for many organizations.

My considerable experience has been in the long-term gain demonstrating that they definitely have their place, *and* they can be tremendously useful, both for individuals and organizations. But you can't just throw anything out there and expect to reap the reward, you need to follow the six strategies for success.

The Six Strategies for Success

This is something I am a fanatic about. *If* policies and procedures are in place, *and* you want them to be successful in delivering some or all of the possible benefits to your organization, then they need to be:

The Six Success Strategies
1. as simple as possible;

2. as short as possible;

3. as usable as possible;

4. as current as possible;

5. written always with the person who will *use* them in mind; and

6. effectively implemented and embedded in the organization.

When policies and procedures are seen to fail, it is almost always because one, or more, of these criteria have not been met, rather than because they are inherently bad or a waste of time, or any other excuse normally given.

And so, as we look to developing your policies and procedures, these six strategies are what we are going to strive for every step of the way.

In the following chapter we need to address the elephant in the room, you guessed it… the dreaded *"Why Me? Why am I the one that has to write these policies and procedures?"*

Why Me? Why am I the one that has to write these policies and procedures?

I would love to have received a dollar every time I've heard someone who'd been given the task of developing policies and procedures say, *"but why me? Surely there's someone else that could do this better than me?"*

In the following chapter I help you ask a different question, *"Why not me?"* I promise you, there is a system to everything, even writing policies and procedures. When you know how easy it can be, you'll be glad you did, and you'll be the hero of the organization.

You can download free resources from the author here
www.howtopoliciesandprocedures.com/resources

CHAPTER 2

*Why Me? The Policy and
Procedure Lifecycle*

**The *Policy and Procedure Lifecycle* will determine who should
develop them**

We've already established that the most probable reason you've
picked up this book is that some policies and procedures need
to be developed, and you're no expert, but you are apparently
supposed to do it.

*Policies and
procedures have a
life of their own - the
question you need to
ask yourself is "Where
do you fit into it?"*

Sarah's story

I was once contacted by the Chief Financial Officer of an organization, Sarah. Within her portfolio, she had overall responsibility for Finance, Human Resources and General Operations and she reported directly to the Chief Executive Officer (CEO).

As you can imagine, Sarah had a huge workload and was overloaded both in tasks and responsibilities. She had just come from a meeting with the CEO where she was asked to develop a full suite of policies and procedures for the organization. The CEO's rationale was, as Sarah's overseeing responsibility covered a number of the areas needing to be documented, and she wrote excellent reports and other business documents, she could be relied upon to take on this extra work and deliver.

Sarah was nearly incoherent on the phone, and although I didn't come outright and ask her, I think she may have been in tears. She had realized what a huge task she had ahead, and she wasn't sure she was up to it. She placed a call to me as she knew I consulted in policy and procedure writing and asked me if I had any templates she could use or look at to get her started. I immediately said that I did, and that of course I would be happy to make them available to her. We then had a discussion around what she needed to do, and I talked through the time commitment necessary, the potential issues of not producing a robust set of documents, and whether she would, in fact, be able to produce these.

The question we ended our conversation on was, "Although the CEO has asked you to do this, are you actually the best person to be doing this work?" And if the answer was no, then did she have any other options?

Sarah left that conversation to ponder those questions, and I sent her a few of my base templates for her to consider. A few days later, I heard back from Sarah saying that she had convinced the CEO that she was not the right person for the job, and they had found some budget to get a consultant in to undertake a project to develop and implement a suite of policies and procedures. She would oversee the project and realized that she still had to commit time and effort to the development, but she was much, much happier than during our previous conversation.

Sarah asked if I would like to tender for the work. I did and won the tender.

A short couple of months later, this organization had a full organizational suite of policies and procedures, documented, trained, implemented and fully handed over to them. Five years later, they still have and maintain this suite of documents, and I've had feedback from both the CEO and CFO that had they not done the project utilizing a consultant, they know the suite would never have materialized to be the productive tool it is now.

Writing policies and procedures is a skill, but that's not the only thing you need to weigh up when deciding whether or not you, or someone else, should develop them. There are a number of factors when you come to make your decision as to who should develop them, and we can explore these by looking through the Policy and Procedure Lifecycle.

Potentially there are different people at different stages of the Policy and Procedure Lifecycle who might be a better fit than you.

Policy and Procedure Lifecycle

You may need to write brand new policies and procedures from scratch, or there may already be something in place that you need to review and update. The Policy and Procedure Lifecycle shows that all policy and procedure documentation is developed and then goes through a number of phases over its lifetime.

▶ The documents may remain in use and circulation for a long time

▶ They may be updated from time to time and then

▶ They may eventually be retired

See the Policy & Procedure Lifecycle diagram, with further information regarding each stage in the table below.

THE POLICY & PROCEDURE LIFECYCLE

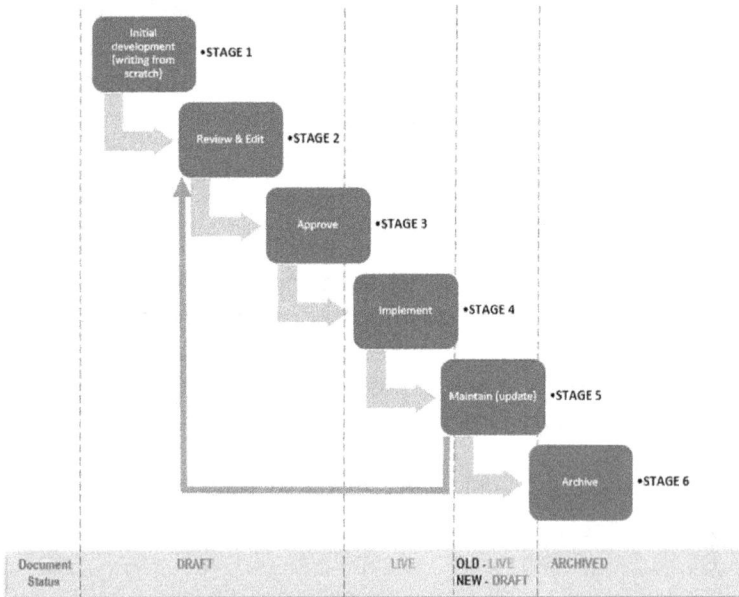

STAGE		Stage Description	Document Status
1	Initial Development	When you don't have a policy/procedure at all in place, and need to develop one from scratch	The document immediately becomes a *Draft*
2	Review & Edit	Once the document is drafted, it will require at least one review and edit, and this review depends on the stakeholders involved	The document remains in *Draft*
3	Approve	Once the document has been approved and is good to go	The document moves out of *Draft* and becomes a *Live* document
4	Implement	Once the document is good to go, it needs to be implemented. People need to see it, read it, become familiar with it, trained in it, and in some cases sign that they have read and understood it and agree to abide by it. And then they need to do it, i.e. follow the rules in the policy, or follow the steps in the procedure	The document is *Live*

STAGE		Stage Description	Document Status
5	Maintain & Update	At some stage, the document ceases to be current, something will change somewhere with something, and the document will need to be changed	At this stage a new version of the document becomes a *Draft* and this new version goes through most of the cycle again (in most cases the first stage of developing from scratch is not required)
6	Archive	When the new version of a document is accepted to go live, the old document will then be archived	The old version usually remains *Live* until the new one is ready for release, and then becomes *Archived*

Now, if we think back to poor Sarah's predicament, told by her CEO that she was now responsible for developing a *full* suite of policies and procedures for the organization from *scratch*, no wonder she rang me in desperation for a bit of help.

Looking at the Policies and Procedures Lifecycle, she was at Stage 1, with absolutely nothing in place.

Stage 1: Initial development:

This is the Big One!

Writing policies and procedures from scratch is a skill, and as such, can be developed with practice, experience and effort. But, and it's a huge but, in addition to the skill required, a person tasked with the initial development of policies and procedures needs time, and the ability to focus on the task at hand.

No matter how skilled they may be, the task requires chunks of time even if an excellent template is used as a basis. More importantly than time, focused attention on the task at hand is required. It is not the kind of task that can be carried out while battling interruptions or breaking up the task with meetings and phone calls in between. This was the crux of the discussion I had with Sarah. Remember the story of our CFO, Sarah earlier in the chapter.

We needed to ask:

- ✓ did she have the skills already on board?

- ✓ more importantly, could she carve out chunks of time to devote to the project?

- ✓ could the organization afford to have her spend time and focus on this project, rather than her other duties?

The answer was a resounding no, the task of writing a complete set of policies and procedures for an organization would require weeks of uninterrupted time. Her job as CFO gave her very little uninterrupted time, and everything else, including her sanity, would undoubtedly suffer because of it. Sarah and the CEO were able to acknowledge this from a conceptual standpoint and needed no further convincing.

As we saw in Sarah's case, quite often the task of initially developing policies and procedures falls to the manager, or the person responsible for a particular area, however, it doesn't necessarily follow that the person in the role has well-developed logic writing skills required for these kinds of documents. And if they don't have these skills, the question then becomes:

▶ Is developing these skills a good way for this person to spend their time?

▶ Does this person have the capacity to develop these skills?

▶ What is the quality of these documents likely to be?

In Sarah's case, she did have the capability to develop the skills, but did not have them at the time. This would add additional time to the project while she developed those skills, and the CEO was on side when pushed about producing quality documents first time around, so that they would be more easily accepted and embedded into the organization.

The CEO did not want to buy trouble further down the line with poorly documented policies and procedures.

When I go into an organization to develop policies and procedures, it's usually when the organization has recognized the benefits and importance of having them in place or have a specific need for them. They have also generally recognized that the money spent on an experienced external consultant would actually be less than the cost of the effort and consequential lack of effort on that person's core business, of having the internal people responsible for that area write them. Or they recognize the importance of implementing high quality documented policies and procedures. Or they are influenced by a combination of both reasons.

There are other reasons you might get an external consultant in. If you're lucky enough to find someone that also has skills in business processes, then as they document your procedures they are able to shine a light on processes that are less than efficient, or question why things are done the way they are, often leading to more effective procedures and clearer, precise policy. Being external, and with a wide range of experience, they may be able to see what you can't, and this has the potential to provide great insight and new ideas into the organization, as well as 'best practice' concepts.

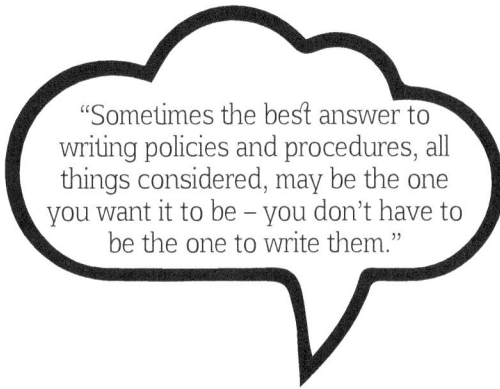

> "Sometimes the best answer to writing policies and procedures, all things considered, may be the one you want it to be – you don't have to be the one to write them."

Larger organizations may implement the idea of an external consultant by having an Organizational Development Team that covers business processes, or a policy writer position. These positions or teams traditionally sit outside the business areas and so can fulfill the external consultant role for other business areas within the organization.

Stages 2-6: the remaining LifeCycle:

In practice, I've found that once a good foundation has been developed, the internal people responsible for the area can usually maintain and update, even with significant changes, with relative ease, without having to dedicate huge chunks of time and with just a modicum of expertise. In Sarah's case, once the project to set up the full suite was complete, Sarah and the CEO have easily taken on maintenance and update of the documents, and a few years down the track, they are still happily updating them as required, or in accordance with their review schedule.

There is one time when I would recommend seeking specialist assistance and that is when policy and procedure need to be developed or changed because of legislative changes or the introduction of new legislation. Often, internal staff do not have the expertise to 'translate' the new legislation/changes to legislation into an internal policy and procedure and have a level of comfort that they are correct in their translation. Finding a person who specializes in that particular area, and not just in developing policies and procedures, sometimes even getting legal advice, may be prudent for an organization.

An example of this was a project I turned down some years ago. I was asked to write a policy and some procedures for the implementation of the new workplace health and safety legislation. I had absolutely no content knowledge of this area and had not even worked in industries where attention to this was already commonplace (for example, construction). I advised the organization that I did not have enough knowledge to be able to translate the legislation into policy. As this area is bound by law, there are serious repercussions if you don't get the policy right, and I didn't want to be the one to potentially put the organization in a precarious position. A few years later, I was called back by the same organization and was able to update these documents when a new regulation was introduced, as by that time I had had much exposure to the legislation and subject area in the intervening years.

If not you, then who?

In all conscience, I must point out that there are benefits to people internal to the organization writing and developing their own policies and procedures.

- ✓ The main benefit is a feeling of ownership and responsibility for them.

- ✓ It will be a shorter development process because your team are familiar with what is working and not working in the organization. You know your systems and what is lacking.

✓ Sometimes, the act of writing what you do and how you do it, can assist you to be critical at the same time, and may lead to improvements, or a deeper understanding of what you do, and why you do it in a particular way.

✓ Also writing them means that you become intimately familiar with the content through the development process.

Generally speaking, if someone internal to the organization is going to write policies and procedures, then they have to know their subject matter, and be in a position to be a decision-maker in what they're writing.

Policies:

Senior management level is usually best suited for writing policies as they are primarily the 'rules' needed for a subject area. Senior managers know the rules and are able to make decisions around those rules, or at least make respected recommendations regarding those rules, to the decision makers.

Procedures:

Procedures are generally best documented by those who actually carry out the work (not the manager that oversees the work as so often happens), so they can provide the level of detail needed for step-by-step instructions.

Sarah's story continues...

Besides not having enough time, and her other duties suffering if she wrote the whole suite of policies and procedures, was Sarah really the right person for the job?

✓ she had responsibility in the organization for Finance and Human Resources and was able to advise in policy for those areas. However,

✓ for the procedures, the bookkeepers and other clerks knew the ins and outs of the day-to-day procedures required.

✓ for the Service Delivery area, she had absolutely no idea about much of it.

Sarah, of course, knew what her organization did and the services they provided, but had no intimate knowledge of these. So, the answer to the question is a resounding NO. Sarah was not the ideal person to write the policies and procedures, that's why they approached me to write them.

In our next Chapter, I'll introduce you to my process for writing policies and procedures. Even if you're not the best person for the job, you might be the only one available. So, let's get into the 'how to.'

The moral of the story here is that time spent at the start of any potential policy and procedure project considering the possible options of who might be able to develop policies and procedures, and choosing wisely, is time well spent.

CHAPTER 3

It's Just a Process – Policy & Procedure Development Process

Sometimes, even when you're not the best person skills-wise, you might still have to write policies and procedures. And sometimes when you have to write them, you should not really be writing them as you have no idea about the content of what you're writing. Unfortunately, in these instances, the reason you shouldn't be writing them doesn't change the hard reality that you just have to do it. And when you do end up writing them under these circumstances, you may not be able to produce a quality deliverable and achieve the benefits you wanted.

It might take time, but it's simple: listen to people and follow the process.

Lucy's story

One of my clients, Lucy, found herself in this very boat. Lucy was the Training Manager for a childcare organization, that was also a Registered Training Organization (RTO), that is, they were accredited by the government to teach and train early childhood educators. Lucy was solely responsible for this arm of the business and to gain government accreditation had written a full suite of policies and procedures, complete with very impressive process diagrams. From where I stood on initial scrutiny, she had done a wonderful job - they looked and read to my childcare-education-uneducated mind like they were really thorough, and well crafted.

And even though they were all that, I was brought in because they weren't working. No one was following them and things that were supposed to be happening (and were covered in the procedures) were not happening. Lucy was stumped as to why and was worried that their accreditation status might be under threat as an audit was looming. I was brought in to review them. So, I did what I do, and started by looking through the existing material. I then interviewed people to learn more about the policies and procedures. I talked to Lucy, members of her team, members of other teams that crossed paths (for example, the Accounts Team in the Finance Department who were involved in charging and collecting student fees) and even the General Manager (Lucy's boss).

At the conclusion of my review, one thing was clear.

The process Lucy had followed, while producing something of quality, had not been robust enough to produce a deliverable that was usable.

1 **Firstly,** Lucy had put together the policies and procedures in a bit of a rush to gain accreditation. Lucy was smart, she had the time, and she had great writing skills. She was also highly organized and structured in the way she approached things, and because some things weren't even being done yet, Lucy had created the documents according to how *she* thought things should run.

For example, the first cohort of students was still halfway through their course when she wrote the Student Graduation policy and procedure. Lucy had written the Sales procedure (how they marketed and sold courses to potential students) as a structured and regimented procedure, as she would like it to be if she was doing the role, and not taking into account that the type of people attracted to these roles are not necessarily going to be as structured as she is.

So, the policies and procedures were not written primarily with the audience they were intended for in mind, and some had been written in advance.

2 **And the secondary point** that became clear was that Lucy's idea of implementing the policies and procedures was to print them off and place them in a folder, and advise all staff that they were there and should be read and followed. Because Lucy was highly motivated to know the policies and procedures and abide by them, she assumed everyone else would be too.

Lucy talked about them in staff meetings, but no training took place of current staff, and no induction happened for new staff. I will cover this point in detail later in the book – no matter who develops the documentation, and how good the documentation is, it still has to be effectively implemented.

Six strategies for success.

If we remember back to our Six Strategies for Success, Lucy, with her excellent writing skills, had managed to make them:

- as simple as possible;

- as short as possible; and

- as current as possible.

But they had failed miserably because Lucy hadn't ensured they were:

- as usable as possible;

- written always with the person who will *use* them in mind; and

- effectively implemented and embedded in the organization.

At the time, I shared a process (and some rules) with Lucy. I undertook this process to perform the review, and they not only passed the audit, but together we firmly embedded the new policies and procedures, so that they are now used as the basis to train new staff and are continuing to keep their registration current. You can follow this process too, so you don't find yourself in Lucy's shoes!

The Policy and Procedure Development Process

Outlined below is the process for developing all policies and procedures, whether from scratch, or for existing ones under review.

The Policy & Procedure Development Process	1. Gather & Familiarize with Existing Information
	2. Review & Agree Standard Formats
	3. ~~Talk~~ Listen to Everyone
	4. Develop Draft Document(s)
	5. Review by Subject Expert
	6. Prepare Final Draft
	7. Approval
	8. Handover/ Implement/ Embed

Let's look at the *Policy and Procedure Development Process* steps in more detail

1. Gather & Familiarize with Existing Information

► Identify who might know about existing documentation

► Gather all existing documentation (policies, procedures, forms, templates)

► Familiarize with existing documentation and identify any gaps and any that need work to bring in line with best practice

The first step is the easy bit. Gather as much of the current documentation that you can find. Anything at all that exists. You will need to consider who in the organization might know, and then ask people where to find the information and how to get it. This includes: all official policy and procedure documents that might exist or have existed, even if they're not current; any unofficial documents, like that scrap of paper in my drawer that was the catalyst for the bookkeeping procedures; any forms that are in use, or have been in use – these will be needed anyway to support procedures, but they can often give great insight into actual procedures as well.

You will need to review all of this material. Have a brief look through it all at the start of the project. Not only will it impact on how and what you deliver in the end, you might be able to use some of it. You need to understand what is in place now, what has been in place previously (that's relevant), what works and what doesn't, and why things are in place the way they are.

> **Rule:** Never ever, *ever*, 'reinvent the wheel' if you don't have to. If you can find something and reuse it, then do so.

2. Review & Agree Standard Formats

- ▶ Identify who will approve/agree to use the standard formats (it might be you)
- ▶ Agree a standard for every possibility, including policy documents, procedure documents, forms, templates, numbering and naming formats, folder/manual/overall structure

Once you have started to familiarize yourself with the material you've gathered in Step 1, you will also be able to begin thinking about standard formats. It's important to commence this step right at the start of the process so that your new work on the documents will be in the correct format, and to minimize rework for you, and confusion for others involved, later. We will discuss the basic formats and what you need to consider in detail in Chapter 5.

In practice, Steps 1, 2 and 3 can happen simultaneously, that is, you start to look through any existing information and while you do that, you can think about the structure and format of what is needed to be developed. You will be talking to people about what exists and what does and doesn't work, including structures (for example, are they too long, not enough detail / too much detail, etc). This information all feeds together to help you make some decisions about standards and formats.

> **Rule:** Take or make a start point. Having somewhere to start is always better than having to start from scratch. So, if you don't have a template for something, then find one. There are hundreds of templates to be found on the internet.

Spend time up front at this stage, analyzing them and then make an informed decision for your starting point. In Chapter 5 we will look in detail at some basic templates and explore what you should be looking for.

3. ~~Talk~~ Listen to everyone

- ▶ Identify who currently knows about the topic area, who sets the rules (policy) and who does the work (procedures and forms)

- ▶ If you are not the subject expert, then identify that person(s) and ask for their commitment to be interviewed, answer queries and then review and approve what you put together

- ▶ Setup and conduct interviews to discuss the documentation being developed (you may have multiple interviews depending on the amount of information being discussed and the complexity of the processes)

This step is particularly important if you are not the subject expert. It is possible for you to write policies and procedures, and design forms, for topics that you don't know too much about, however you will need to talk to the people that are, and rely on their expertise. You need to know things like: who does the work now; how the work is done; what are the steps they take; where it goes after they've finished with it; what forms or other tools and systems do they use; and what are the bits and pieces on the forms that work or need changing.

If you are the subject expert, then of course you'll be able to write the bulk of it without interviewing anyone else. But don't make Lucy's mistake – talk to, and more importantly listen to, people in your team, other people that do the same jobs or are affected or impacted in some way by what you're writing about, and talk to your manager to get their view. Most of the talking you'll do will be in the form of questions about the processes you are describing, for example, "What happens then? And what happens with that form? How does that get from there to there?"

After you've finished listening to them and have gathered as much information as you can about their processes, you need to explain a couple of things and ask for their commitment.

1. Explain the process you're going to follow (pretty much this process) and what the rough timeframes are going to be.

2. Explain that even though you are putting the bulk of the documents together, you will still require some time, focus and commitment from them, and that this will likely have some impact on their other work. This is to answer any further queries you might have, and also to review what you put together. Explain that this is essential to help the documents be as accurate as possible and for a successful implementation.

3. Ask for their commitment as appropriate – to help out by reviewing what you've done, to review and approve what you put together, etc.

> **Rule:** The success of this stage lies with you and your frame of mind. You need to both be, and appear to be, non-judgmental of those you are interviewing, and open to what they have to say.

You need to *be* non-judgmental, because you need to keep an open mind. One thing I've learned is that things develop a certain way for a reason, and you may not necessarily find out what that reason is, and people can get defensive about this. But you also never know what you might turn up – some parts of what they do and how they do it may actually be excellent, or they may have innovative ideas that haven't been implemented.

You need to *appear* to be non-judgmental, because when people advise you of what their process is, or their procedure, it can be experienced like a mini performance appraisal for them. It can seem as if they are putting forward their work, what they do, why they do it, and how they do it, to you for evaluation. If they get even a hint that you judge them, and worse, are found wanting, they will clam up. They will probably keep answering your questions but will give you no further information and certainly not share any of their own ideas or thoughts or opinions. And if they do feel judged by you, you may as well kiss goodbye getting their commitment to help and then following through on that commitment.

4. Develop Draft Documents

▶ For existing documentation perform a systematic review of each organizational/topic area (e.g. finance, governance, etc). Check every document and make amendments to the content if necessary, and format in accordance with the (new) standard documents

▶ Create new documents for any gaps that have been identified

▶ Discover the true audience for the documents and write for them (acknowledge there may by multiple audiences)

This is the step that will take the most time and focus. It's where you will draft all the necessary documents, and draft forms, and work other tools into the documentation. You'll need to immerse yourself in the task and cut out interruptions as much as you can.

In Chapter 5 we are going to look in detail at the development of each different piece of documentation: policies, procedures and forms. For now, just remember the Six Strategies for Success will be the foundation of everything you develop.

Whatever you write needs to use 5 of the 6 strategies:

1. As simple as possible – you will edit every document, every section, every item, every sentence to have no flowery descriptions or extra words or anything that is a 'nice to have'. Every single sentence you write will inform the reader of something that it is absolutely essential for them to know.

2. As short as possible – see above. In addition to this, you will try as far as possible to keep information in manageable chunks. Documents that are pages and pages long are a

big no-no, sections that are many lines long are also a no-no. If everything in a document is essential, but you still end up with a long document, think about how you can break it up into more manageable chunks. For example, if you have a very long procedure, with many steps involved, consider breaking it into two or three procedures, or sub-procedures.

3. As usable as possible – the aim of every document you produce is to make it easy to use. While this may seem obvious, the use of elements such as font formatting, headings and sub-headings, paragraph numbering, bullet points and common formats (or templates) used across multiple document types; can all make or break the usability of your documents. We'll talk about this in more detail in Chapter 5 where we explore the different documentation types.

4. As current as possible – when you're in the process of developing policies, procedures and forms, it is the time to ensure that they are as current as possible. By talking to people (Step 3 above) you will gain an understanding of what is happening now. Taking into account current legislation and regulations for the topic area, as well as general research on the latest thinking around the topic, can all help.

5. Written always with the person who will *use* them in mind – the last but most important! Although there may be many people who refer to and use your documentation, if you write your documents for the person who is new to it all, and knows nothing about the topic area, you will cover all bases. Develop to the level of detail that a person, completely new to the organization, can pick it up and do the job they need to do with it

"Communication is key. Even when developing policies and procedures, the more you communicate, the better and more useful they will be, and the more they will be utilized."

And to support, and help you achieve, all of the above, I'm going to sneak an extra rule in at this stage to make your life easier:

6. Information only in one place. As far as possible, you do not want to repeat information in two policies or have two procedures doing the same steps. For example, if two procedures start to have the same steps, then break off the shared steps into another sub-procedure and then reference the new sub-procedure from the original two procedures.

5. Review by Subject Expert

► Review of every document and provision of feedback as required from the subject expert if there is one, and yourself if there is not

In the case where you are not the subject expert, you will need to call on the commitment that you got from them in Step 3. It's nearly a guarantee, that no matter how thorough you have been in your interviews in that stage, or how expert your interviewee was, that you, or they, will have missed something, or not quite got it right. So, someone who knows the topic must review your first draft, and sometimes there may be more than one person to consult at this stage.

If there is no subject expert, and you are it, then you must also review your first draft. In this case, write the first draft and leave it for a few days, even longer if you can. Don't look at it at all in that time so that you can return to it with 'fresh eyes'. You'll be surprised what you pick up after you've given yourself a bit of distance from what you've written.

The time between drafts should be kept to a minimum. Due to the nature of the work, the longer it is between drafts, the more time will be taken for you to regain your focus and close familiarity with the documentation.

This can be a bottleneck area, as it requires time away from other job activities for the subject expert. To give yourself the best chance of getting quality feedback in a timely manner, you need to be flexible with your approach, and try to make the reviewer's job as easy as possible. You can offer for them to provide feedback in whatever way they find easiest. Some of the ways you can offer to receive their comments are: use a facility like 'Track Changes' where they make changes in the word processor document; use a shared document facility like Dropbox where they can include their comments; allow them to print and then handwrite their comments; and verbally over the phone or in an interview.

6. Prepare Final Draft

▶ Once feedback is received it can be incorporated into a final (second) draft

If your interviewing in Step 3 has been effective, then there should be minimal changes, and this is usually a straightforward process of incorporating the feedback received from the subject expert. Sometimes some rework may be required.

7. Approval by Subject Expert

▶ Once feedback has been incorporated and the final draft prepared, the document returns to the subject expert for final approval if required

If the feedback is straightforward, you can just incorporate it and advise the subject expert it has been done as per their instructions. If there are significant change(s), the document will need to go back to them for a more thorough, second review.

Once the document is finalized, the subject expert will be agreeing that it is approved and ready to be implemented. Again, make their job easy by making any alterations you have made easy for them to find, review and approve. You don't want them going through every line of what you've written again.

8. Handover/ Implement/ Embed

▶ **Handover** – sometimes you may be just required to handover the finalized document(s) as you've written them for someone else

▶ **Implement** – includes both the initial training for people in how to use the documents and start to become familiar with them, and also the storage and access to the documents

▶ **Embed** – includes paying attention to how new employees are inducted to them as well as how they are maintained from this point on, and kept current and effective

You can write the most simple, short, current policies and procedures and design the most useful forms in the world, but if they are not effectively implemented and embedded, they will not be used.

This is how policies and procedures get their bad reputation. Not necessarily because they were badly written, but because not enough attention was paid to how they would be utilized in the organization, and time spent to ensure this happens. In Chapter 6 and 7 we explore implementation and embedding in more detail.

— ◊ —— ◊ —— ◊ —

From here though, we are going to delve into the nitty gritty of what to actually write in your policies and procedures, and how to write the documents and design the forms.

Remember to download free resources from the author at
www.howtopoliciesandprocedures.com/resources

CHAPTER 4

*An Overview - What to Write and
How to Organize it*

Olive's story

In one of my most difficult policy and procedure assignments I was originally engaged to write an Operations Manual for a team, within a department, within an organization. I had developed a similar manual, in conjunction with Olive, the team's manager, while she was in a different organization, so she and I both thought we knew exactly what was needed. Olive was quite new to this organization though, and when I came on board, I was bombarded by everything that was currently in place. This organization had everything, and I mean everything. Things I had not ever seen in practice before!

> *You can't help but get off to a great start if you just get the basics right and keep it simple.*

They had policies, procedures, documented processes, process diagrams and work instructions. They had Operations Manuals, they had Process Manuals, they had Policy Manuals and they had Procedure Manuals. They had process management software and a document management system, and they had documents floating around everywhere.

I understood why Olive needed help.

As I tried to get my head around everything, I understood why Olive wanted another manual for her team.

- No one could find anything; things were documented two or three times in different places.
- Her team on the ground, who were just trying to do their job, simply found the forms they needed and saved them locally to their computers and told each other verbally what they needed to do with them.
- This was a perfect example of how policies and procedures get a bad name.
- Everyone blamed the documents saying they were unusable and vowed they would never use them!

It took me some time to sort through what was there, and I also used this time to understand the different stakeholders' agendas.

✓ Olive just wanted a compact easy-to-use procedural manual specific for service delivery within her team.

✓ Olive's team were divided, with staff thinking their workarounds were working, so wanting no change or introduction of new documentation.

✓ Team leaders responsible for inducting new staff, and managing the performance of their team members, saw the benefits a manual would provide.

✓ Then there was the team responsible for the upkeep and management of the process management computer system who wanted to remove the system but replace it with something else.

✓ Finally, the newly appointed Quality Assurance Manager who was aghast at the sheer volume of documents and systems and just wanted to sort out everything they already had before embarking on something new.

On my recommendation, we agreed to proceed with a bit of everything – in an orderly fashion. I set about drafting an Operations Manual for Olive's team, and I also provided a basic structure for the fundamental building blocks of what could be their policy and procedure 'system'

Phew! I imagine you feel pretty tired just reading this – I know I felt tired having to sort it all out. In fact, Olive's story was one of the catalysts for me to write this book, no one should ever have to go through that, including me.

moving forward, as well as some basic templates. (The Operations Manual then referenced new policies and procedures created as I went, using new templates).

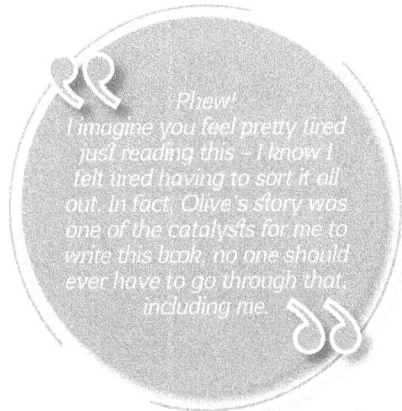

The QA Manager had already started and was encouraged to give priority to documenting what they had, where it was and whether it was current and usable, with the plan to move things across over time.

Resounding success.

The project was a resounding success, although still with much work to be done. The reason for declaring it a success was that we had identified a way forward that would work within their organization and satisfied all the stakeholders' different agendas. This included specific 'operations' manuals to allow teams to access just the information they needed, while referencing separate policies and procedures and accessing ones that were common across different teams and departments.

A simple, underlying structure for both the documents and the 'system' to manage these documents was designed. It now didn't matter about the technology - what software platform was used or how the documents were stored (whether in a document management system or not). Whatever tools might be chosen in the future would simply implement the structure we had agreed upon. Even the QA Manager was happy as he was able to put together a migration plan for the current documentation mess to the new 'system'.

Fundamental structure

While every organization is different and has different requirements, there is a fundamental structure that can be used at least as a starting point for most organizations. This is the structure I used with Olive's organization, and I have used it countless times since.

Let me be clear, this is just one way of doing things, there are others. There is no one right answer or one best solution – there may in fact be many. Provided the one you choose, or design covers the basics, it doesn't actually matter which one you go with. The key is to pick one and run with it, and then *stay* with it.

Normally I would work from the top down, but I'm going to build the structure for you from the bottom up. The full structure will then make more sense as you can see how everything hangs together.

Starting from the bottom

When dealing with policies and procedures the simpler the base is, the better. To keep it simple we only have three things to worry about:

1. Policies

2. Procedures and

3. Forms

At this stage we won't worry about how these are documented or what system is being used, I want you to think about them more as concepts.

Policies

A **Policy** documents rules. It states rules and guiding principles for a topic, describing *'the way things are done around here, and why they're done that way'*

Policies establish broad principles and frameworks that govern an initiative. They should outline all the **rules** for the subject area, and the **principles** behind the rules (the spirit of the rules). They may be strategic (regarding the aims, goals and mission of the organization) or operational (relating to the administration and management of the organization).

Procedures

A **Procedure** outlines instructions to implement rules, or step by step instructions to implement guiding principles. They describe *'how things are done around here'*.

A procedure expresses a *policy* in action, or how a *process* needs to be done. It provides specific instructions to carry out an activity/task and may be stand-alone or be one in a sequence of procedures that comprise a larger activity. Procedures may need to adhere to specific 'rules' and reflect principles from one or more policies.

Please note:

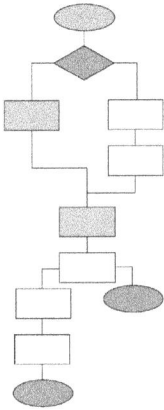

You might have noticed that I've mentioned yet another "P" word – Process. So, what's the difference between a process and a procedure? A process is a high-level flow of linked activities, which once completed, will accomplish an organizational goal. Some organizations choose to implement Processes as one of their document types, however, this adds another level of complexity to something we are trying to make as simple as possible. So, they have not been included in our structure. Process diagrams, which visually represent the steps and decision points of a procedure, can be utilized sometimes to assist in documenting procedures.

Forms

A **Form** puts into practice instructions, rules and guiding principles (from policies and procedures).

Relationship between Policies, Procedures and Forms

All three share the same aim – they exist to enable organizational goals, and all co-exist in order to achieve this goal. If a document or a form exists that is not tied in some way to an organizational goal, then someone has had too much time on their hands, and it is not needed (remember keep things simple and short). The diagram below describes the possible relationships between each, and the tables explain some guidelines and provide examples.

```
POLICY          POLICY          POLICY

- - - - - - - - - - - - - - - - - - - - - - - - - - - - - - - -

        PROCEDURE          PROCEDURE
           PROCEDURE

- - - - - - - - - - - - - - - - - - - - - - - - - - - - - - - -

   FORM             FORM             FORM
```

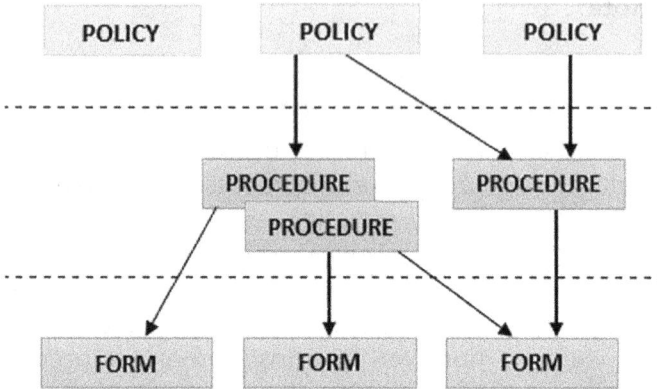

Policy <> Procedure

A Policy may 'own', or refer to, one or more Procedures	**Example:** The Recruitment Policy may 'own' the Job Advertising Procedure and the Interview Procedure
A Policy may have no Procedures attached to it	**Example:** No specific procedures may be required for an Access & Equity Policy as these principles will be implemented in different functions in the organization
One or more Policies may refer to the same Procedure	**Example:** Both the Payroll Policy and the Financial Expenditure Policy may refer to the Employee Expense Reimbursement Procedure

Policy <> Form

Because Policies don't contain instructions on how to do something they don't 'own' Forms, however sometimes a Form may be referred to in a Policy	**Example:** The Financial Management Policy may refer to the Insurance Register form

Procedure <> Form

A Procedure may 'own', or refer to, one or more Forms	**Example:** The Petty Cash Procedure may 'own' the Petty Cash Reimbursement Form
A Procedure may have no Forms attached to it	**Example:** The Office Security Procedure may have no forms required to implement the procedure

Holding it all Together

If you develop policies and procedures for an organization or even just for a team or yourself, you are going to quickly find that there are numerous documents to keep track of. Just as you need a simple base, you are going to need a simple way of organizing everything. You might be lucky that you have a system that will organize everything for you, even so, you will have to first tell the system how you want things organized. Again, there are no right or wrong answers, and this will provide a start point for you.

The diagram below shows the two main concepts we will detail that will allow you to organize your policies and procedures effectively.

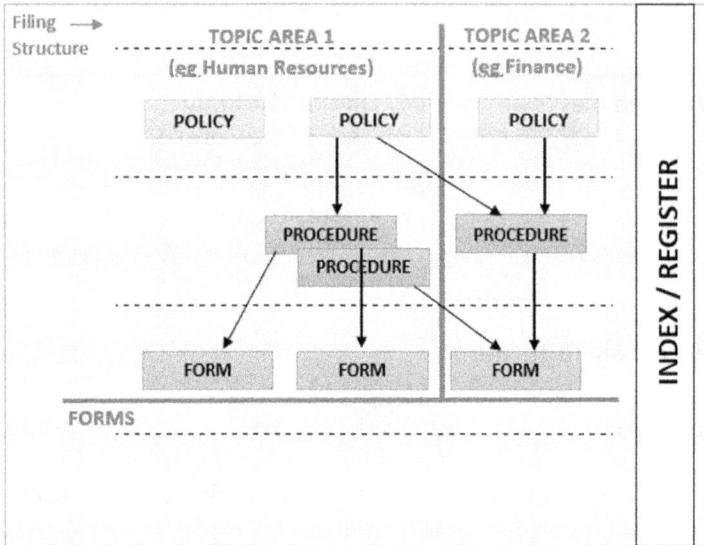

Filing Structure

The filing structure is indicated in red in the diagram and is about sorting how the documents are accessed by the people who use them.

1. Policies and procedures are divided into Topic Areas (or functional/operational areas). Generally, there will only be a handful (under 10) topic areas. All policies and procedures pertaining to one area are grouped under their Topic Area, meaning that each policy and procedure has to fit under a topic area. This also makes it relatively easy to allocate a person responsible for each category, for approval or drafting of policy and delegating procedure writing and maintenance.

2. No further categorization is done, as this just makes it more complex to find documents. The filenames of the documents are sorted alphabetically in each Topic Area.

3. You will notice that Forms are in a separate area and not located with their procedures. The reason for this is usability. When people use forms, or are trying to locate them, they don't want to have to think about where the form comes from or 'belongs'. For example, if they are trying to locate an Annual Leave form to apply for time off, they don't want to have to think about whether it is a Human Resources form or a Finance form, they just want to find the form that's for annual leave.

4. Sometimes individual policies can be ambiguous as to where they fit in the structure, and a decision will have to be made as to best-fit. For example, a Code of Conduct for an organization may be located under Human Resources as it is a code for employees, or it may fit better under Governance as it pertains to all the organization and how the organization is run. The key to your decision here is to place yourself in the shoes of the people using the documentation, where would they naturally expect it to be?

An example to get you started

The categories or topic areas are loosely based on the organizations structure, for example a filing structure for a typical organization may look something like this:

Category	Description
Finance	Contains all Finance related policy and procedures
Governance	Contains all policy and procedures related to the overall governance of the organization, for example, Code of Conduct Policy, as well as Vision/Mission/Values statement, etc
HR	Contains all Human Resource (staff and volunteer) related policy and procedures

Operations	Contains all policy and procedures related to the running of the internal organization, for example, Information Technology Management, Research & Development Policy, etc
Risk Management	Contains all policy and procedures related to managing risk within the organization, for example, grievance and dispute resolution, complaints policy, privacy
Client Services	Contains all policy and procedures related to the delivery of service. For example, Customer Service Policy, Infectious Diseases Policy, Case management Policy, etc
WHS	Contains all policy and procedures related to work, health and safety
FORMS	ALL forms and templates for ALL categories are stored in this folder

Note: Abbreviations should be used as they are commonly used in the organization. In the above example, Human Resources is known by the abbreviation 'HR' so the filing structure uses this same abbreviation. Another organization may not have HR at all, but use 'People and Culture' or 'P&C' or 'People Services', so replicate the terms or abbreviations commonly used in your organization.

Policy Register

Some sort of an index or table of contents structure is essential to get an overall picture and assist in locating documents, particularly for those people involved in the administration of your policy and procedure documentation. An example from our earlier case study of the development of an Operations Manual for Olive's team, is where the Quality Assurance Manager had to manually search numerous systems and documents and filing structures to compile a full list of policies and procedures and forms.

"I'll bet your work is already complex enough, so don't overcomplicate your policies and procedures - simple documents, simple structure, simple life - that's the aim anyway!"

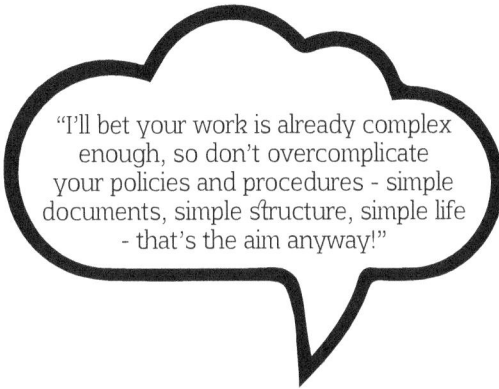

It needs to be some sort of list that gives an overview of policies, procedures and forms, and you may choose to have a number of these registers, depending on different sets of users. People that fulfill a role similar to our Quality Assurance Manager, might need a complete policy index, firstly in alphabetical order and then sorted into Topic Area. A spreadsheet can be useful for creating a Policy Register. However, for Olive's team, they had a conventional, customized Table of Contents within their Procedural Manual which contained only those documents they utilized.

Tools and Systems

There are two kinds of tools and systems to talk about here. Firstly, a tool or a system used to help you manage your policies, procedures and forms, for example, a business process management software tool. Decisions around how documents are accessed by the people who use them, and how to assist people to locate specific documents, will rely on what system you are using.

Obviously, a paper-based or manual electronic system is no/ low-cost and easy to implement. With this method, significant consideration must be given to the organization of the documents. This is key to the usability of the documents. The harder it is to locate a document; the less likely people will use them. And when a manual system is used, an effective implementation and maintenance approach is vital to manage the documents. We will cover this in Chapters 6 and 7.

If your organization has, or chooses to purchase, a specific system to manage policies and procedures, there are numerous document management and process documentation systems on the market. These systems usually handle implementation and maintenance effectively – things like version control, for example, will be automated. However, no matter if these systems are used, the organization of the documents still needs to be designed effectively.

> Even if a very fancy online process management system is purchased and used, if the information itself contained in the system is not usable, then the system won't help!

And in some cases, like we saw with Olive's organization, it may even exacerbate the problem of people not taking up and using the policies and procedures.

The second type of tool or system that needs mentioning is one that your policies, procedures and forms may interface with. This would be anything used to assist in performing a task/activity, for example a software system used for payroll. It's important to be mindful of the relationships between the tool and your documents, when developing your policies and procedures:

- One or many policies, processes or procedures may reference a tool

- Tools may need to adhere to specific 'rules' and reflect principles from one or more policies

- Tools may need to reflect procedure instructions and/or process flow

For example, if your Payroll policy states that all timesheets must be approved, and the Payroll procedure advises that the supervisor is the person that must approve their team's timesheets, then when using a payroll system, this rule may be automated with employees submitting their timesheet for approval to their supervisor. Only once the supervisor has approved it does it then become available for the Payroll team to process the payment.

It's only once we know how we will organize all the information, that we can then drill down into specific detail for the concepts regarding policies, procedures and forms. So, let's go there now in Chapter 5.

Remember to download free resources from the author at www.howtopoliciesandprocedures.com/resources

CHAPTER 5

The Devil is in the Detail

Paul's Story

One organization that I work with had an extremely serious complaint lodged against Paul, the CEO, from a person external to the organization. I was brought in to manage the complaint and Paul assured me that they had an entire, and current, Policy and Procedure Manual for the organization. As the organization was a service delivery organization, they had a Complaints Policy and Procedure in place. With this support, I felt comfortable accepting the assignment. My first inkling that things were not going to go exactly to plan, was when I received the paper copy of the complaint which was done as a large dossier, 137 pages to be exact! I asked if there was a Complaints Form that would assist people making a complaint to think through and present their complaint in a structured way, and which would in turn assist me as I started to deal with the complaint.

> *Structure, simplicity and consistency are the key concepts at every level and it's not hard to achieve these if you know what you're doing!*

You guessed it, there was no such form, but that's okay, I didn't start panicking at that stage – it's not the end of the world – you don't need a Complaints Form, it just might have made things a bit easier.

I turned myself to becoming familiar with the Complaints Policy, and the procedure I would need to follow. Very soon it was apparent that even though it looked the goods, the manual was completely inadequate. The primary issue was that the Complaints Policy and Procedure was written as one section, with no clear delineation between policy and procedure. All of the information about dealing with complaints was jumbled together. In addition to this, there were no clear 'rules' about whether Paul should be stood down during the investigation, or even what an investigation should entail. All the information was written freeform, without many headings or sections or numbering – it was just a few pages of writing divided into paragraphs that I had to wade through to try to find instructions and policy direction statements. There were ambiguous statements that could be taken as a rule, or as a suggestion for how something might be done. And as someone new to the organization, and the Complaints process, I certainly could not pick it up and seamlessly deal with the Complaint from start to finish, in an integrated way.

On top of all of this, the information that was there was extremely hard to navigate through, as the Complaints policy and procedure was not a separate file, but was contained as one section in the Human Resources Policy which was over 200 pages long. There were links to other policies such as the Privacy Policy, with no hyperlinks, so I was forever losing where I was, searching for things with particular words I would have to remember, and was continually moving around the huge document.

And so, what was already a difficult complaint for Paul and others involved, due to the nature of the issues, turned out to be more than double the work. I not only dealt with the complaint itself but had to formulate a proper procedure for dealing with it as we went along. As there was very little policy direction written into the document, there were no prior established rules, so I had to check the rules with everyone involved as we went along. The organization paid for this in real terms, by paying me for all the extra time, but they also paid for it in terms of increased pressure on Paul, other management and on staff. The good news for the organization was that I documented a discrete Complaints Policy and a Complaints Procedure while we undertook the investigation and resolution of the current complaint and they were able to exit the process with a new and vastly improved way of dealing with complaints.

In the previous chapter we were talking about structuring and organizing your policies and procedures to make them more usable. To assist in usability and keeping them short and simple, individual documents and forms will also have an internal structure, something this organization's policies and procedures clearly lacked. There are a number of shared elements common to *all* documents that we will explore first, and then we'll look at the internal structure of each document type in turn. Examples of how all elements are implemented in practice can be found in the document templates provided in Chapter 6.

Shared Element 1: Separation of Policy from Procedure

The main issue with the usability of the Complaints Policy and Procedure in Paul's organization, was that there was no separation of the concepts for Policy and Procedure. Many organizations have a 'Policy and Procedure Manual' and in this each topic area has just one document where policy statements and procedural instructions are all mixed in together. Some even incorporate the form in the document as well.

Separating these as concepts, even if they are together in the same document, is really important, for a number of reasons.

1. Policy is generally fairly stable (policies do not normally change every few months, and while they do need regular review, do not generally need to be particularly flexible). Procedures on the other hand use the rules described in policy to describe how something is done and so are more 'living' documents. Staff need to be able to follow procedures, and to do this, they need to be up to date.

2. Along similar lines, splitting the concepts safeguards the policy and any changes to the rules, while allowing flexibility for procedures to be changed as and when needed – particularly if they are stored separately as well (for example, in separate documents).

3. From a practical perspective of using and reviewing documents, one document that contains both policy statements and procedural documentation can become long and unwieldy for everyday use, and much harder to edit at review time. And it is quite common that the policy document will be reviewed and edited by a different person/role than the procedures associated with it, so keeping these separate assists in simplifying their maintenance.

4. Version control is tidier as you can have numerous iterations of procedure without the policy having changed.

Shared Element 2: Document Owner

To ensure your policies and procedures are implemented effectively, and also maintained and kept current over time, every document will have an organizational role allocated as the responsible person for the document, known as the 'Document Owner'. For example, the Document Owner for the Leave Application Procedure might be the HR Manager if they are responsible for mapping out the process for applying for leave in an organization. If changes need to be made to the process, the person in this role will make them, or at least be responsible for getting them made. In many cases, the Document Owner will be the same as the subject expert we talked about earlier. Some hints for assigning Document Owners to documents:

1. Always record a position title as the Document Owner, rather than the name of the person who is in that position at the time. The obvious reason being that as people leave the organization, change roles, etc you won't have to update the documents

2. Forms don't require a Document Owner as they hang off a procedure (so the responsible person for the procedure also owns any forms used for the procedure)

3. The Document Owner information should be located in the document somewhere, so that if a person reading the document has questions or seeks more information, they know who to contact

Shared Element 3: Unique Identifier

Every document, policy, procedure and form should be given a unique identifier which is a number exclusive to that document. No one really cares what the number is, or what it looks like, it's just useful for administration purposes, for example, to search for a particular document. Some organizations, however, use their unique identifiers as a type of shorthand, particularly for forms, as in you will need the A20 form to apply for annual leave. This is not intuitive for the person trying to locate the form, and they will need knowledge of the exact number of the form to locate it, rather than being able to search for 'Leave Form' using the example above. Some hints for implementing a unique identifier for all documents:

1. If a more sophisticated system is used, the documents may be allocated an internal unique identifier which you may not even be able to see, but in manual systems the unique identifier must be allocated by hand and written into the document somewhere. And it should be recorded in the Policy Index or Register that you use to keep tabs on all your policies, procedures and forms.

2. Place the identifier in a header or footer within the document. And whatever you do, don't place it in the document (file) name, as this should be easy to understand for administration purposes, to find documents that need to be updated or changed. A plain English title for the file name is essential, and alphabetic order is usually more useful when searching.

3. Finally don't place the identifier in the document title within the document as the person trying to use the document doesn't need to see or use the ID. For example, someone searching for the Leave Application Form will

search for just that. They don't want to have to know and remember that they're searching for 'HR001F: Leave Application Form'

4. In a manual system, as well as a unique number for the document, it can help to have a system to better identify the individual documents, for example, a letter/ letters designated for each topic area and one for the type of document (i.e. policy/ procedure/ form). For example, a unique identifier for the Leave Application Form may look something like: **HR001F**; which is made up of the following:
    HR signifies 'Human Resources' content area;
    001 is the number of the document within the topic area; and
    F is the type of document, i.e. it's a Form.

*   If you use a system such as this, the abbreviations for functional (or topic) areas will match those used in the filing structure, see the example table below.

Functional Area	Abbreviation
Human Resources	HR
Finance	F
Governance	G
Workplace, Health & Safety	WHS
Service Delivery	SD
Operations	O
Information Technology	IT
Marketing	M
Risk Management	RM

- Wherever possible use and abbreviate the name of the functional area as used in your organization. So, for example, if your Finance function in the organization is known as Financial Management, then your topic area would be 'Financial Management' and your abbreviation would be 'FM'

- To identify document types, wherever possible use the first initial of the word to keep it simple. Except if there are two starting with the same letter (as you can see below, policies take the 'P' and procedures goes with the second letter 'R').

- Note that in the above table we have an 'F' for Finance, and in the table below, there is an 'F' for Form. In our example this is okay, as one will be at the start of the unique identifier signifying in which functional area the document belongs, and one will be at the end, signifying the type of document;

Type of Document	Abbreviation
Policy document	P
Procedure document	R
Forms	F

- It can also be useful to match the number of each document. In our example above, the process for applying for leave in an organization has a procedure and a form – so we assigned the Leave Application Form the unique identifier HR001F, so the 'Leave Application Procedure' will be allocated the unique identifier 'HR001R'.

Shared Element 4 : Version Control

To ensure ease of use and maintenance of the documents, every document should be labelled with a version number. This allows the organization to ensure that the most current version of the document is in use.

"Sharing is caring... Even when developing policies and procedures."

1. A more sophisticated document management system will take care of version control automatically. In a manual system, it can help enormously to have a system for versioning documents. For example, a simple manual versioning system may comprise of just two levels and a status indicator, in the filename or title of the document:

Level	V1	Indicates this document is Version 1 and reflects a wholescale edit or review of the document *Document Filename V1*	Placed at the end of the filename, the V indicates Version, and the number following is the document version number, 1 being the first version, 2 being the second version of the document following a wholescale review, etc
	V1.1	Indicates this document is Version 1.1. and reflects a small modification has been made to the document that does not change the intent of the document or significantly alter content *Document Filename V1.3*	Placed at the end of the filename, the V indicates Version, and the number following is the document number, followed by the number of small modifications that have been made to the document
Status	**DRAFT**	Indicates the document is in DRAFT status and is not a live document *Document Filename V1 DRAFT*	Placed at the end of the filename (following the version number). The absence of the word 'DRAFT' indicates the document is 'live' and in use EG: Leave Application Procedure V1.1 Leave Application Procedure V1.1 DRAFT

2. Version numbers in a manual system may be located in the document, and file names may also include the version number, as per **V1 or V1.1** as this will make them easy to reference and find the correct one when needed. For example, the following filename "*Leave Application Form V1.1*" helps identify that the person seeking this form is using the correct version.

    Note that some file systems will rely on the filename when you create links to documents and placing the version number in the filename may not be sustainable. For example, if a procedure document references a form to be used, then it is good practice to not just reference the name of the form, but to provide a link to the actual form in the procedure document. When someone wants to access the form, they simply click on the link from the procedure and this opens up the form. If your system relies on filenames used in the link, then each time you update the form and then change the version number in its filename, you would need to find the link in the procedure document and update it.

3. During editing and reviewing, the addition of **DRAFT** at the end of the filename may be used to assist during modifications as per, **V1.2 DRAFT** (indicating this document is a draft of the new version V1.2). For example, "*Leave Application Form V1.2 DRAFT*" easily identifies the new version that has not yet been approved to be released.

Shared Element 5: Links to other Information

In Chapter 4, we snuck in a rule which says that information should only ever be in one place and that we don't repeat the same information in different documents. The rule in this context means that any references to other documents or information should be included in the content as a hyperlink. This goes for internal and external information or references. For example, relevant information from a different internal policy will not be regurgitated in this document but referred to with a link to the document. Reference to a piece of government legislation should be a hyperlink to that legislation on the internet (and you will not usually copy the information from an external source and paste it in your document).

Shared Element 6: Consistency of elements between document types

To the extent possible, keep these shared elements consistent between document types. For example, if the unique identifier for procedures is located in the bottom right hand side of the footer of the procedure, then the unique identifier should be placed in the same position for forms and policies, and formatted in the same way. This way if a reader is looking for the unique identifier in any document, they know exactly where to look, and for a new person, becoming familiar with one document type makes it easier to become familiar with other document types.

And keep other common elements found in each document type consistent and in line with other organization design standards to enhance usability. These might include:

1. **Fonts used** – Limit your font used to one standard business-style font such as Calibri or Arial for all documents and don't mix fonts within documents. Use bold and italics and different font sizes for headings and to differentiate text

when required. And use these differentiators consistently. For example, if you decide that a sub-heading will be Calibri font, size 12, bold – then every sub-heading across all document types will be formatted in this way.

2. **Color** – Prudent use of color is acceptable. We don't want bright yellow headings that no one can read on the screen. However, if you wanted to provide some visual prompts and use a red colored 'X' and a green colored tick to indicate things that are acceptable or not acceptable, then this might be a good idea. But just because I've said it's okay to use color, don't get carried away! Lots of color and poor choices of the use of color can lead to a very distracting document.

3. **Terms used** – Use relevant terms consistently and correctly. Use terms commonly used in your organization within your documentation and use them consistently. For example, if you refer to the people that you provide services to as 'customers' in your organization, then always use this term, don't mix it up and use other terms such as 'client' or 'service user'.

— ◊ —— ◊ —— ◊ —

These common elements help to form part of the structure which makes policies and procedures as simple as possible to use and maintain. In this same way, individual elements found in the different document types can also be consistent within the document type, and we'll look at these in the next chapter.

Remember to download free resources from the author at www.howtopoliciesandprocedures.com/resources

CHAPTER 6

No Excuses - Use a Template

Remember Lucy at the Childcare Education Training Organization? We've already picked apart what she didn't get right the first time around, causing the need for an external consultant (me) to review them and implement them over again. But let's give credit where credit is due. She did one thing that saved her organization a considerable amount of money, time and effort, and that was utilize a template for her documents.

> *Taking a step back and designing common templates will allow you to move forward faster and with ease.*

When I came to revise the documents, it was a significantly simpler exercise to review each document and tweak as required or rewrite due to their format and style being consistent across all documents. The time taken during training for implementation was considerably shortened, as team members became familiar with the template format very quickly and were able to read and utilize the documents in an increasingly short period of time. An extra bonus for Lucy was, that following my review I provided feedback to the CEO that the documents were sound and robustly usable. The CEO made the decision to roll out the template that she had created across other departments of the organization.

Be like Lucy and design and decide on a template for policies, procedures and to the extent possible, forms. Using a template means that when you then create policies and procedures from them, deciding what information to put in those documents becomes a bit of a 'no-brainer'. No thought is necessary, or time wasted trying to decide what to put in the document, as you just fill in the template. It also means that updating and maintaining them are easier as all your documents will be consistent. Importantly, the readers' experience of using multiple documents becomes much easier, as they are able to become familiar with new documents much more quickly and easily as they become familiar with the template structure. They can focus less on trying to find information, and more on the content of what they require at the time.

There are many templates and examples available on the internet for you to have a look at to see what might be included or not, and to help you decide how your template might be formatted. I've included a template and have picked apart each different document type, explaining each template for you.

The Policy Template

The most important thing with writing policies is to try to increase the likelihood that they will be referenced and used, so keep them short and to the point. No big chunks of flowery descriptions of principles and background information that no one is ever going to read. No extraneous sections at the beginning of the policy document so that the reader has to scroll through three pages before they even get to the relevant bits!

I have included a simply formatted Policy Template below where simplicity and usability is the goal. The table describes the sections necessary for a basic policy document. This Policy template can be found on my website, 'Simple Procedure Template'.

<<POLICY NAME>> POLICY

INTRODUCTION

<<Insert the background information on why this policy exists using Black Calibri 11.>>

PURPOSE

<<Insert what this policy seeks to achieve. >>

SCOPE

<<Who does this policy apply to? Any other points regarding the scope of the policy. >>

POLICY

1. Insert the actual content of the policy; the principles the policy is based on, the details of the position held by the organisation on the topic.
2. Use simple numbering to easily identify policy points
   2.1. And sub-points
3. Indicate internal policy references as per: XXX Policy
4. Indicate internal procedure references as per: YYY Procedure
5. Indicate internal form references as per: ZZZ Form/Template

Sub Headings
1. A policy document may include several sub-headings under this topic, depending on the complexity of the policy matter.
2. Sub-headings will be Calibri font size 12, black, bold.

DEFINITIONS

Term	Definition

CONTEXT

Internal Documents	• List of internal documents related to this policy
Legislation, Standards, etc	• List of external legislation or government regulations, etc relating to this policy. Include a link to a website for easy access.

DOCUMENT CONTROL

Number	???	Approved by ???? on	
Version	Version 1	Scheduled review	MMM YYYY
Responsible	???		

Policy Document Sections	
SECTION	**COMMENT**
Header	▪ Options are to either keep it blank or include the title of the document and/or a small organization logo formatted according to preference (left, center or right justified). The advantage of having the document title in the header is it is on every page, in a consistent and noticeable position. Note: the simple template provided has no logo and the document title is not included in the header. ▪ In larger organizations, you may choose to include the logo of the department as well
Introduction	The background information of *why* this policy exists
Purpose	Describes what the policy seeks to achieve
Scope	▪ Describes who (what roles in the organization) the policy applies to ▪ Describes any other points regarding the scope of the policy, or what it covers. For example, you might have an Accounting Record Keeping Policy that is specific and only covers financial records (not employee records or client records)
Policy Statements	▪ This is the detail of the policy, describing the position held by the organization on this topic (the view of the organization, the rules around it that the organization will enforce) and any principles the policy is based on ▪ Use of headings and sub-headings in this section are essential to break the information into logical and manageable chunks for the reader

Definitions	▪ A table for definitions at the bottom of the policy document is recommended. Including definitions in the text of documents becomes very messy, and makes the content more complicated to read and understand. And don't place the table of definitions at the top of the document, as we just want to get straight into the content as soon as possible and not have to scroll through a page of definitions just to read the policy statements ▪ It's a personal preference whether to have the borders of the table visible ▪ Text for this area is in dark grey, to distinguish it from content of the policy when a reader is scanning the document ▪ The table may not be required if you have a system that has functionality similar to an online dictionary where you can just click on a word or hover over it, and it displays the definition from there (and your policies are going to primarily be accessed online, rather than in hard copy)
Context	▪ This section is a table which describes the context in which the policy sits – any internal or external references to other policies, legislation, etc that influence the organization's policy ▪ Text for this area is in dark grey, to distinguish it from content of the policy when a reader is scanning the document ▪ This table is optional, alternatively each reference can be included wherever they are mentioned in the document content

Document Control	• This section is a table which describes the information about the document (for example, the unique identifier and the Document Owner) • The table has very light grey background shading to set it apart from the content of the policy • Rather than having all this information on the footer of every page, and so repeated, it's included as a section in this template as it is only needed once in the document. However, this is a preference item and some organizations may prefer to have this information in the footer so that it does appear on every page of every document
Footer	The footer should contain only information that you need to see on every printed or viewed online page of every policy document, so in this template: • The Policy title (if it's not prominently in the header), so that the reader can easily see which policy document they are in. Optional to include with the policy title is the topic area name, so for example you might reference the policy title as such *Human Resources: Annual Leave Policy V1*. Then you know exactly where it's come from as well • The unique identifier can also be placed in the footer, for accessing the document, so the title may be referenced as such *Human Resources: Annual Leave Policy V1 - HR001P* • Page number of the document, with a preferred format of *Page X of Y*, so that the reader knows where they are in the policy and how many pages there are (especially when looking at a printed copy) • Sometimes it can be useful to place a statement about printed copies, such as *Printed copies are uncontrolled: date of printing dd/mm/yyyy*, which signify to the reader that the document was printed on a particular date and may not be a current version • Text for this area is in mid-dark grey, to make it as unobtrusive as possible when reading the content of the document, but it's there if you need it

Some other Policy Design Considerations

In addition to using a formatted policy template, there are two additional considerations for designing policies.

"Don't make it hard for yourself later. Set up your templates and then go, go go!"

Firstly, within each topic area, you have a choice to create one overarching policy that contains everything that pertains to that topic area, or you can create many specific policies. In the Human Resources functional area, for example, you may choose to create one *'Human Resources Policy'* which outlines all of the areas within the one policy document, or you may choose to create a separate policy for each distinct area within HR, ie Recruitment Policy, Performance Management Policy, Discipline Policy, etc.

While having one umbrella policy document is usually a tidy and simple way of arranging policies for your topic areas, particularly if you are a small to medium sized organization, your choice may be swayed by a number of factors:

?   Is there so much content for the topic area that having one umbrella policy will make it difficult to read, use, implement and maintain? In this case, it would be a valid decision to separate the policies for ease of use and maintenance reasons.

?   Are there potentially different 'owners' for these areas? For example, in a larger organization, you may have a Recruitment Manager who is specifically in charge of Recruitment and 'owns' this policy and someone else in charge of Employee Experience who 'owns' Performance Management and Discipline. In this case, separating the policies allows two different people to be responsible for their respective areas.

?   Does the system you are going to use to manage and store all the information work more effectively with many separate policies?

If the decision is to have one overarching policy document, then formatting and the use of headings and numbering are paramount. Frankly, they are essential in any case. Over anything and everything else, no matter which way you choose to go, *conciseness is key*. Use of bullet points, no flowery descriptions and no unnecessary segues between sections will all help in the document's usability.

The second important design consideration is to pay attention to the terms you use to indicate that something is a rule, rather than a guideline or a recommendation. The use of the following in policy statements: *must* vs *should* vs *shall* vs *will* should be considered. In most cases it is recommended that *will* be used (*must* sounds a little draconian, *should* suggests there is a choice and *will* is forward-looking and more positive than *shall*).

The Procedure Template

> The most important thing for writing procedures is to write with the reader (the user of the procedure) in mind.

And the reader you should be targeting is the one who is completely new to the procedure, for example, a new employee in the organization. They should be able to pick up the document, start at step one, and continue until the job is done without getting too overwhelmed. Discretion is vital in structuring procedures to ensure procedure documents are not too large and onerous. If they become that way, they need to be logically grouped and split accordingly.

This is the reason that when we look at the different sections in the basic procedure template below, we do away with all the extraneous sections as these are just superfluous words that nobody reads when using procedures. The reason someone accesses a procedure is to figure out how to get something done, so by the time they have found it, they just want to go straight to the first step and start doing what they need to do.

Speaking of superfluous words, there are a lot in the table below. This is because most of the sections are replicated straight from the Policy template (same content, formatting, location, etc). These sections are marked in dark grey in the table below and if you've read through the Policy Document table, you're in luck and won't need to re-read them here. While it's unquestionably important to keep these consistent between the document types for ease of use for the reader; for your ease, right now, skip straight to the Procedure Statements section.

The Procedure template can be found on my website, *'Simple Procedure Template'*.

<<PROCEDURE NAME>> PROCEDURE

PROCEDURE

1. Outlines how the policy is implemented on a day-to-day basis
2. Use simple numbering to easily identify policy points
   2.1. And sub-points
3. Indicate internal policy references within the text, as per: ⬛ XXX Policy
4. Indicate internal procedure references within the text, as per: ⬛ YYY Procedure
5. Indicate internal form references within the text, as per: ⬜ ZZZ Form/Template

Sub Headings
1. In the event sub-headings are useful, they will be Calibri font size 12, black, bold

CONTEXT

Internal Documents	• List of internal documents related to this procedure
Legislation, Standards, etc	• List of external legislation or government regulations, etc relating to this procedure. Include a link to a website for easy access.

DOCUMENT CONTROL

Number	???	Approved by ???? on	
Version	Version 1	Scheduled review	MMM YYYY
Responsible	???		

Procedure Document Sections	
SECTION	COMMENT
Header	■ Options are to either keep it blank or include the title of the document and/or a small organization logo formatted according to preference (left, center or right justified). The advantage of having the document title in the header is it is on every page, in a consistent and noticeable position Note: the simple example provided has no logo and the document title is not included in the header ■ In larger organizations, you may choose to include the logo of the department as well
Procedure Statements	■ This is the detail of the procedure. With this directly under the Header, there are no introductory sections and the document just launches into the steps of the procedure immediately ■ Tidy and well-formatted content/steps are critical in these documents ■ Tables are used to capture a high level of detail, many steps and/or multiple roles responsible for different steps ■ Use of headings and sub-headings in this section are essential to break the steps into logical and manageable chunks for the reader

Context	▪ This section is a table which describes the context in which the procedure sits – any internal or external references to policies, other procedures, legislation, etc that influence the procedure ▪ Text for this area is in dark grey, to distinguish it from content of the procedure when a reader is scanning the document ▪ This table is optional, alternatively each reference can be included wherever they are mentioned in the document content
Document Control	▪ This section is a table which describes the information about the document (for example, the unique identifier and the Document Owner) ▪ The table has very light grey background shading to set it apart from the content of the procedure ▪ Rather than having all this information on the footer of every page, and so repeated, it's included as a section in this template as it is only needed once in the document. However, this is a preference item and some organizations may prefer to have this information in the footer so that it does appear on every page of every document

Footer	The footer should contain only information that you need to see on every printed or viewed online page of every procedure document, so in this template: • The Procedure title (if it's not prominently in the header), so that the reader can easily see which procedure document they are in. Optional to include with the procedure title is the topic area name, so for example you might reference the procedure title as such *Human Resources: Annual Leave Procedure V1*. Then you know exactly where it's come from as well • For accessing the document via the unique identifier, this can also be placed in the footer, So the title may be referenced as such *Human Resources: Annual Leave Procedure V1 - HR001R* • Page number of the document, with a preferred format of *Page X of Y*, so that the reader knows where they are in the procedure and how many pages there are (especially when looking at a printed copy) • Sometimes it can be useful to place a statement about printed copies, such as *Printed copies are uncontrolled: date of printing dd/mm/yyyy*, which signify to the reader that the document was printed on a particular date and may not be a current version • Text for this area is in mid-dark grey, to make it as unobtrusive as possible when reading the content of the document, but it's there if you need it

Some other Procedure Design Considerations

In addition to using a formatted procedure template, there are two additional considerations for designing procedures.

1 Sometimes a procedure can get very long! Or part of a procedure may be referred to by other procedures. In these cases, splitting the procedure into two or more procedures will be essential. This will not only assist in usability, but also save you from repeating the same information across two documents (remember the rule that wherever possible, information is only in one place). With our Annual Leave example, you might start to document the procedure of requesting annual leave from your manager, and then find that you are also documenting the Payroll procedure of deducting the annual leave days from your leave balance. In this case, it might make sense to create a new procedure for the payroll steps and just refer to the new payroll procedure in your Annual Leave Procedure.

2 Sometimes procedures can get quite complicated. Do this step, then this step, then if this happens do another step, but if something else happens then do a different step. In this case, the inclusion of a Process diagram, which shows the flow of steps can assist the reader to follow the written steps. There are very good process diagram tools on the market, however, unless you use these tools continually, or have time to learn them, this will be an additional overhead for you. Documenting them using the more manual drawing tools in your word processor is definitely a little more time consuming and fiddly, but this should be weighed against learning a new tool and the cost of a new tool. And if you are handing over the documents to a subject expert to maintain, it is highly unlikely they will be able to maintain diagrams produced in a specialized tool easily and without a lot of extra effort.

A Form Template

Designing forms is its own craft, and one of those things that is hardly noticed when it's done well, but when done badly is highly irritating for the person trying to use the form. Each form will be quite different in what it needs to capture, so a template or standard format for the bulk of the form may not be possible, but there are still some elements of form design that are useful to keep in mind.

- Consider the primary usage of the form (will it be filled in online or on a device or printed and filled in by hand). This will influence the use of dropdown boxes, etc.).

- Does the form mimic a process and if so, what is the flow (for example, one person fills in one part, then another person fills in another section, and then it goes to a manager for approval). Facilitate the process flow in the form design (separate, clearly marked boxes for each person in the order in which it will be filled out, signature section at the end, etc).

- Include instructions. In practice, forms are implemented processes, procedures and policies. Facilitate the use of the form by simple instructions, and as far as possible implement a standardized way of including the instructions so it becomes easy for people who use many forms to find them (for example, the instructions are always written at the top of the form, or they are always written at the top of a section, etc.). The example Form Template provided below has instructions in a smaller, italic font and situated immediately underneath the form title. A copy of this template can be found on my website 'Simple Form Template'.

- Consistency is key
  - ▶ Develop a standard for formatting fields and descriptors to capture information. For example, all form information is formatted in a table, with borders, descriptors are always in bold and with a ':'. In the Form Template, this is demonstrated by the use of the Arial font, bold and using ':' to denote a field descriptor.

  - ▶ As far as possible have standardized areas of forms, with a section header and using a different weight of borders around the areas, and perhaps even using colors to separate these. For example, a Customer Details section shaded in blue, and always placed at the top of all forms that collects details on the customer. For all forms that record customer details, this section is included, but the fields required may be different according to the details needed for that form. Another common example is a section for internal processing – an area at the bottom of the form to be used once the form has been filled in and returned and now needs to go through some internal checks or approvals. In the Form Template, a standardized approval section has been included and denoted by a light shade of yellow.

  - ▶ Pick one font and stick with it (use bold, italic, size and color to highlight text for different purposes). As used in the Form Template example provided, Arial is useful as it displays well on the screen and on paper, is clear and you can also utilize Arial Narrow to make use of a smaller font (say for instructions), when space on the form is at a premium.

  - ▶ Standardize whatever else you can across forms, for example, if the form heading will be all capitals, then all form headings are always capitals. This example is used in the Form Template example provided.

▶ Having said that consistency is key, you may choose to have two slightly different templates – one for forms used internally to the organization, and one for external use. For example, you may choose to have the organization's logo in the header of the external form template, but may decide you don't need the logo for internal forms.

While a form template is difficult to provide due to every form being so different, there are still some standards that can be implemented on a template, as per the Form Template and the table below. The sections marked in dark grey are again replicated straight from the Policy / Procedure template (same content, formatting, location, etc).

(••) Logo

Name of Form

Instructions: Employees are to fill all sections and sign, then send to Supervisor for approval and signature.

Date:

Employee Name:		Title:	
Supervisor Name:		Title:	

INFORMATION	
Field 1:	Field 2:
Field 3:	Field 4:

MORE INFORMATION	
Field 5:	Field 7:
Field 6:	Field 8:

APPROVAL

Employee's Signature: _____ Date: _____

Approved by: _____ Date: _____
(Supervisor)   Signature

                          Print Name

Form Sections	
Header	• Options are to either keep it blank or include the title of the document and/or a small organization logo formatted according to preference (left, center or right justified). The advantage of having the document title in the header is it is on every page, in a consistent and noticeable position. Note: the template provided has a logo but not the form title in the header • In larger organizations, you may choose to include the logo of the department as well
Main Section	This will be dictated by that information required on the form and what it needs to capture
Footer	The footer should contain only information that you need to see on every printed or viewed online page of every form, so include: • The Form title (if it's not prominently in the header), so that the reader can easily see which form they are using, such as *Leave Application Form V1*. Optional to include with the Form title is the topic area name, so for example you might reference the procedure title as such *Human Resources: Leave Application Form V1*. Then you know exactly where it's come from as well • For accessing the document via the unique identifier, this can also be placed in the footer, So the title may be referenced as such *Human Resources: Leave Application Form V1 - HR001F* • Page number of the document, with a preferred format of *Page X of Y*, so that the reader knows where they are in the form and how many pages there are (especially when using a printed copy) • Sometimes it can be useful to place a statement about printed copies, such as *Printed copies are uncontrolled: date of printing dd/mm/yyyy*, which signify to the reader that the form was printed on a particular date and may not be a current version

Footer	▪ Text for this area is in mid-dark grey, to make it as unobtrusive as possible when using the form, but it's there if you need it
	▪ One final option that can be considered is if the form is used externally to the organization, some statement regarding copyright or confidentiality of the form might also be appropriate, for example using the statement "© Organization Name YYYY" to indicate the organization claims copyright of the form

— ◊ —— ◊ —— ◊ —

Spending time deciding your templates before you start work on the documentation itself is time well spent. You will be armed and ready to go, able to focus solely on the content of the documents and comforted by the knowledge that there will be no need for rework. The documentation will get easier to write as you become familiar with the template setup and take less time for each new document. In a similar way, spending time upfront thinking about how you're going to store and file the documents is an investment of time you won't regret, and that's what we'll look at next.

Remember to download free resources from the author at www.howtopoliciesandprocedures.com/resources

CHAPTER 7

If it wasn't for people,
implementation would be easy

I know I keep coming back to Lucy at the Childcare Education Training Organization, and here we are again, as implementation was the main issue with her policies and procedures. As we've already mentioned, her policies and procedures were very well-written, well formatted using templates, easy to follow and had process diagrams to die for. And all for nothing, as no one in her team used them. Printing off a copy, putting them tidily in a clearly marked folder and showing people where they can find them if they need them does not cut it for implementation, and Lucy found this out the hard way. Nobody used them and she found herself with a team of people all operating in the way they thought was best.

> *Paying attention to people and paperwork is the key to successful implementation of your policies and procedures.*

For example, she had designed and written a robust sales procedure, which she knew from personal experience worked to increase sales. It ensured that initial contacts to the organization were followed up and given a special discount offer, this was followed up by a phone call where the sales person then recorded the reason if they chose not to sign up with them for a course, to see if they could improve their offering. The sales process that actually developed while this procedure sat in the policy manual folder, was that some of the people taking the initial calls would follow up with the discount and some wouldn't, some would pass on the potential customer's details for follow-up and some wouldn't, depending on the on-the-job training they had received when joining. Naturally sales were suffering because of this. It was only after our review project and ensuring an effective implementation, that the sales procedure Lucy had designed was fully understood, accepted and adopted by her team. Sales immediately started to improve post-implementation.

That's why it's included as one of the six strategies for success for developing effective policies and procedures.

There are two parts to implementation, the easy bit and the hard bit. The easy part is the system, that is, implementing the documents and forms so that people can access them – in a filing system on your computer system or comprehensive document management system or even hard copy manual. The hard part is the people part – training people to use them and start to become familiar with them.

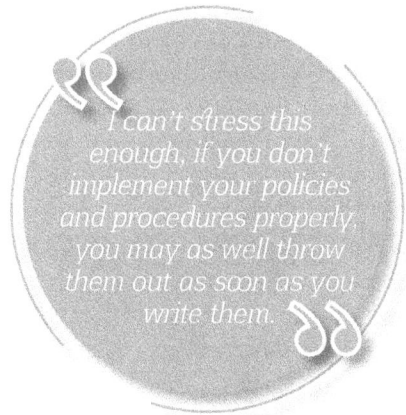

> I can't stress this enough, if you don't implement your policies and procedures properly, you may as well throw them out as soon as you write them.

Let's tackle the easy part, system implementation, first as this has to be in place before you start trying to figure out the people part.

System Implementation

I may have made a rash statement by saying that the people part of implementation is the hard bit, because some document management systems or organizational setups are quite challenging. If this is you, or your organization, unfortunately you may have to follow whatever process is required to implement the documents into your chosen system.

If you have the ability to create your own system, implementing a simple online filing system is the easiest solution.

The Filing System

You will need to create a filing system for storing and using policies, procedures and forms. There are two parts to your filing system:

1. **The 'LIVE' system** – This is for general use by everyone in the organization for the viewing of policies and procedures, and access to form templates. The documents will be stored in a central area in the computer system everyone in the organization can access and will be sorted into the folders according to your functional area categories.

   Remember in Chapter 4 where we talked about the filing structure as a way to help organize your documents? This is what we'll now implement. Using the example from Chapter 4, we would implement a top-level folder and then some sub-folders, in alphabetical order, as per:

📂 **Policy & Procedure Manual**

📑 Client Services

📑 Finance

📑 FORMS

📑 Governance

📑 HR

📑 Operations

📑 Risk Management

Notes

- Your organization might not want to call it a manual, but might call it Policies and Procedures, or give this top-level folder a completely different name

- The sub-folders are usually accessed in alphabetical order, but if for any reason you would like these ordered differently, say for example you would like FORMS to be at the top of the list, just add a number to the start of the name of the sub-folder, ie '1. FORMS', '2. Client Services' and so on

- Notice that all forms will be in the FORMS folder, and the word is capitalized to make it stand out from the topic areas

- If possible, the FORMS folder should be protected as 'Read Only', ie not allowing people to save changes to documents within this folder. This is to ensure that when using the forms, people must take a copy and use the copy, rather than accidentally saving information over the top of the blank form

2. **The Administration system** – For maintenance and administration of the documents, a separate area will be setup which is available only for people with the ability to edit documents and remove and add documents. This will be setup with two sets of filing structures identical to those in the 'live' system, as per:

📂 **Policy & Procedure Manual**	📂 **Policy & Procedure Archive**
📁 Client Services	📁 Client Services
📁 Finance	📁 Finance
📁 FORMS	📁 FORMS
📁 Governance	📁 Governance
📁 HR	📁 HR
📁 Operations	📁 Operations
📁 Risk Management	📁 Risk Management

Notes

- As you might guess, the first one is a copy of the live information, and the second one allows you to move and store old versions of documents as they become superseded.

- You may want to label the archive area so that it sorts to the bottom of the list, for example, Z-ARCHIVE.

Filing in the Filing System

When all the filing system is set up, individual documents can be filed as follows:

Live System:

1. All policies and procedures will be saved as a PDF version (Or other non-editable format) in the 'live' system;

2. Forms will be stored in their editable formats in the 'live' system so they can be copied and used.

Administration System:

1. All documents (policies, procedures and forms) will be stored in the Administration system in their editable version, in their original application (eg Word, Excel);

2. Only documents that are no longer in use, or have been superseded by a new version are to be moved to the Archive sub-folders, and only the editable versions are required to be moved (PDF versions can be deleted).

Implementing the individual documents

Before documents can be filed during any implementation, some attention must be paid to the document itself. Following acceptance by the subject expert of a new policy, procedure or form, the document needs to be updated with Document Control information, for example, the next Review Date. The following steps will be undertaken:

1. In the document, make appropriate changes to the Document Control table, using the template provided in Chapter 6 these would be:

    ✓ **Number:** Check your Policy Index or Register and decide where the document should sit and add it in, and give it an appropriate document identifier

    ✓ **Approved by XXX on:** Add the Document Owner's title (e.g. CEO), and then add the actual date that the document was approved

    ✓ **Version:** update this to reflect the version number. This will normally be Version 1 for a new document

    ✓ **Scheduled Review:** add the next scheduled review date (this is the date that the document should be reviewed to ensure it stays current. We will discuss a policy review schedule in Chapter 8). If there are no special requirements for review, then the month of approval should be used, with two years hence

    ✓ **Responsible:** add the Document Owner's title e.g. CEO, not a person's name

2. **Policies and Procedures:** The document will be added to the appropriate subject/functional area folder in the Administration System (if it's not already there). As it is a new document, it will be named with a V1 in the filename (for version 1);

    a. The document will then be saved as a PDF (or another non-editable format) using exactly the same filename as Version 1 in PDF format;

    b. The PDF file will then be copied/moved to the 'live' system and saved in the same appropriate subject area folder.

3. **Forms:** All forms will be added to the FORMS folder in the Administration system. As it is a new form, it will be named with a V1 in the filename (for version 1);

   a. The form will then be copied/moved to the 'live' system and saved in the FORMS folder

People Implementation

First, let's look at what it means to have effectively implemented policies and procedures.

"Yes, you need to implement the system itself, but it's the people that will be using the policies and procedures that are the keystone to effective implementation."

People in the organization need to know:

- ✓ Where to find them on the 'Live' system

- ✓ When and how to use them

- ✓ If something is wrong with them or needs updating, how, and to whom, do they pass that information on

- ✓ They also need to form part of an induction process so that all employees new to the organization are introduced to them

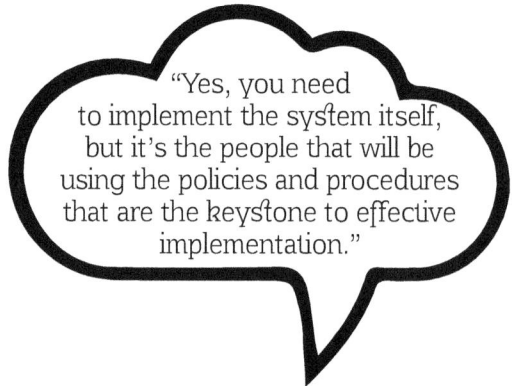

Subject matter experts assigned as Document Owners need to know:

- ✓ All of the above

- ✓ Where the 'Administration' system is and how this is structured

- ✓ What the process is to update them, and their responsibilities in this regard

Get an early start on implementation...

If you've done your job well in the early parts of the Policy and Procedure Development Process (see Chapter 3) then you will have already started the first part of implementation. In Step 3 of the process, well before you've even started writing the documents, you would have talked to a whole range of people about the policies and procedures. Another name for this is consultation. Consultation is fundamental to getting people to not only understand and be familiar with, but also to accept the need for the policies and procedures you've developed, and the forms you are introducing. If you have consulted well, and with the right people, half your work is already done.

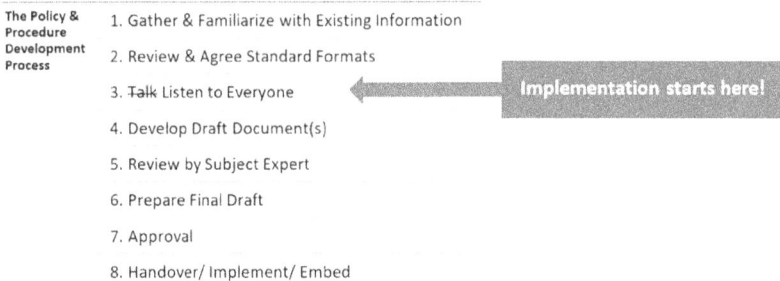

The Policy & Procedure Development Process	
	1. Gather & Familiarize with Existing Information
	2. Review & Agree Standard Formats
	3. ~~Talk~~ Listen to Everyone ← **Implementation starts here!**
	4. Develop Draft Document(s)
	5. Review by Subject Expert
	6. Prepare Final Draft
	7. Approval
	8. Handover/ Implement/ Embed

The rest of the people implementation for policies and procedures is formalizing them and embedding them into the appropriate people's jobs. There are a number of ways this can be done:

1. Handover to the Document Owner (the subject expert) and introduce the notion that they are responsible and accountable for successful implementation and take-up of their policies and procedures. This is the person who should have a vested interest in the success of the documents, so as much as possible involve this person, and have at least some of the accountability for the successful implementation fall on their shoulders

2. Individual team members need to become familiar with the new documents and this can be done in a number of ways:

    > Introduce to a group and present the highlights, for example, in a team meeting

    > If the policies are critical or the procedures are complex, custom training might be required to introduce the documents and how they should be used in the organization

    > Set individuals the task of reading the documents and familiarizing themselves, and then coming back to you to confirm this has been done

    > A sign-off section can be used in individual policy documents to indicate that an individual has read and understood and agrees to abide by the policy, especially when they are extremely important to the organization. For example, with the introduction of Workplace, Health and Safety laws, it is a legal requirement that workers are familiar with the policies and procedures, and their responsibilities under this legislation in the organization they work in. Using a sign-off section can be used to track this

> Training – whether it is face-to-face, or a short video that is distributed to team members, can be invaluable in assisting the acceptance and implementation. In Lucy's case, we conducted a full day of face-to-face training and went through all the new procedures, and then got the team members to practice putting some of the procedures into action.

3. 'Embedding' policies and procedures means that implementation is not a one-time thing, but a continual process, including:

> New people in the organization must also become familiar with them, so including them into the Induction process you have for new employees is essential

> Maintaining them so they are current and reflect both internal and external changes affecting the organization

— ◊ —— ◊ —— ◊ —

Maintaining policies and procedures is outside of the Policy & Procedure Development Process but is an essential component of the Policy and Procedure Lifecycle. Let's look at it now, and then you're all done.

Remember to download free resources from the author at www.howtopoliciesandprocedures.com/resources

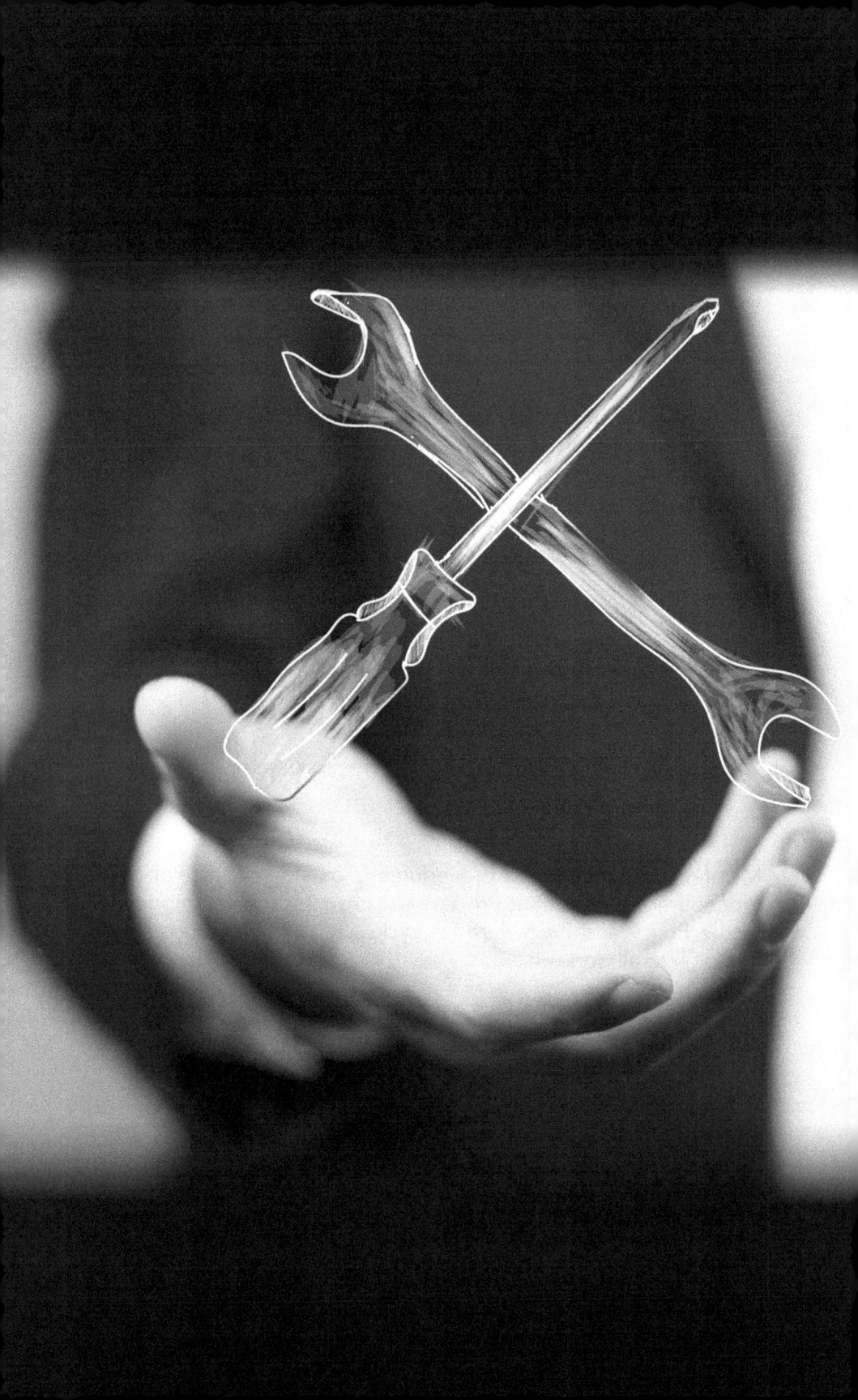

CHAPTER 8

Maintain to Sustain

Maintenance is counted as essential to embedding policies and procedures because it helps to sustain two of our Six Strategies for Success across the lifecycle of the documents, that is, it keeps them:

> *It's really not that hard to keep your policies and procedures neat and tidy and current, and the alternative is all your hard work to put them in place going to waste.*

- ▶ as current as possible; and

- ▶ effectively embedded in the organization.

You might recall Sarah the CFO from Chapter 2 and the organization I developed a full suite of organizational policies for because Sarah wasn't the right person for the job. You might also recall that I mentioned the organization was still maintaining their suite years later. It continues to be incredibly gratifying each time I work with this organization on various consulting projects, to find the extent to which they maintain and utilize them. They have fully implemented a regular maintenance schedule and their Document Owners have taken full ownership and responsibility for keeping their subject areas up to date.

Consulting projects that I have undertaken with them have, as a direct result, been able to keep costs to a minimum, as well as significantly reducing their own time required for these projects. A specific example of this was the introduction of a new Performance Appraisal system for staff. During the initial development of the Human Resources suite of procedures, they flagged this as something they would introduce in the future, and so it was not developed at the time. A few years later, I was brought in to design the system, and then documented the process in the policy and procedure format. They had kept all of the Human Resources documentation up to date and current, so when I needed to reference position descriptions these were up to date. When there was a reference to other relevant policies, for example, appraisal during probation period processes or update other linked documents like the Induction Procedure, all of this was current. This meant that all of the embedding and implementing parts of the current project were simple and took no extra time. It was a pleasure to be able to conduct a discrete piece of work that then fit so seamlessly into their organization.

Sarah and her organization have recognized the benefits of maintaining their policies and procedures and accepted the unavoidable but manageable additional workload for the Document Owners.

> Policies and procedures are not something you can just set and forget. But, when they are living documents that get updated when things change, and reviewed from time to time, they have the potential to save time and effort in other areas and future initiatives.

The documents need to be flexible to evolve, but not many organizations have the luxury of having a person dedicated to maintaining them, so a manageable schedule for review should be put in place.

Policy Review Cycle

All policies usually require a formal approval from one person, or one body of people (for example, the CEO or executive management team, or the board). This is because they form the rules and outline the guidelines, or principles, by which the organization operates. If this is the case, the whole suite of policies can be reviewed over a staggered two- or three-year cycle, and this can be put in place according to a timetable, see below for an example.

Procedures and Forms Review

Procedures are usually more flexible than policy documents and may be updated by the Document Owner as the need arises. Internal forms (which are used by people within the organization) are also usually flexible. And although care must be taken when updating external forms (ones used by clients or customers, etc), it is usually essential that these are kept up to date as the need arises.

"And now for the best bit! We have procedures for your procedures!"

In all cases, a bit of setup work putting in place a simple process to follow for reviewing documentation will pay dividends for you later (so this should be introduced during implementation).

A Procedure for Reviewing Policies and Procedures

The easiest way to implement a review process for the organization is to add to the policies and procedures a document that covers how these reviews are handled. That is, you implement a procedure for reviewing procedures and policies and forms. Here are the basic steps you could start with, and customize for your organization:

1. The subject expert/Document Owner for each subject area establishes and maintains a *Policy/Procedure/Form Change Log* (see below for an example, other columns can be added as necessary.) It can be a very simple document used to record any suggestions, comments or requests for changes to policies, procedures and forms in their subject area. An organization may choose to just have one central log for all requests for change.

Policy Area	Policy/ Procedure/ Form Name	Change Suggestion	Suggested by	Date
Policy area the document belongs in	Document title	Detail of the change suggested	Who suggested or requested the change	Date request received

2. Anyone in the organization may identify the need for a new policy, procedure or form, or for an amendment of an existing document and they will send this via email to the Document Owner.

3. The Document Owner will note the requirement/suggestion in the *Change Log* and decide timing and priority for the change. Sometimes the change may need to be made immediately, and sometimes it can be scheduled for a future scheduled review time.

4. When the time comes for a review, sufficient time must be allocated for consultation with all appropriate persons and bodies, review of related external documents and information, and review of all affected internal policies, procedures and forms. This review will be relevant to the changes needed. For example, if new legislation has been introduced, then this will be a major change and may require significant time allocated for the review. On the other hand, if it's just a handful of small improvements or tweaks, then the review will require much less effort.

5. In general terms the review will follow the Policy and Procedure Lifecycle detailed in Chapter 2 with documents moving from *Live* status to *Draft* and again to *Live* status.

6. When the new document, or the reviewed document, is ready to go, all the Implementation considerations (that we covered in Chapter 7) for the people side of implementation, must be taken into account.

7. You will need to implement the new documents into the document management or filing system that you use. In terms of the manual system, new documents follow the process that we set up in Chapter 7 for implementing individual (new) documents.

8. For policy documents that have been reviewed as part of the Policy Review Cycle (a mandatory review of each policy every 2 to 3 years), if no changes are required as a result of the review, the policy document, Document Control section must still be updated, i.e.:

   ✓   **Approved by XXX on:** Add the date that the changes were approved

   ✓   **Scheduled Review:** add the next scheduled review date. If there are no special requirements for review, then the month of this approval should be used, with two years hence

9. For any documents that are changed, the process will be to:

   a.   Take a copy of the current version from the Administration area on the filing system, and work on the changes in this copy (using 'DRAFT' in the filename). For example, if you are making small changes to the Annual Leave Procedure V1, take a copy of the file, and name this file *Annual Leave Procedure V1.1 DRAFT*

   b.   Once changes are made and approval is received, rename the working file, removing the DRAFT status. In the example above, the new file will be *Annual Leave Procedure V1.1*

   c.   In the document, make appropriate changes to the Document Control section, ie:

      ✓   **Approved by xxx on:** Add the actual date that the changes were approved

      ✓   **Version:** update this to reflect the new version number, in the example, *Version 1.1*

      ✓   **Scheduled Review:** add the next scheduled review date. If there are no special requirements for review, then the month of approval date should be used and two years hence

    d.   Implement as per the process set out in Chapter 7

10. Update the *Policy Index/Register* to reflect the new filename (version number will be different).

— ◊ —— ◊ —— ◊ —

And finally, take a deep breath. You are done.

> Remember to download free resources from the author at
> www.howtopoliciesandprocedures.com/resources

CONCLUSION

The Art of Being Skillfully Boring

Developing and writing policies and procedures is a skill. I would like to say it's an art but I'm just trying to make it sound glamorous because it may be singularly the most unexciting job you can do. Boring, yes. Superfluous or without benefit – no!

The inspiring, touching and humorous story to finish this book with is yours.

> Develop the Art of Being Skillfully Boring.

Let your policy and procedure development be the final product of this book. I hope you are inspired to tackle that policy and procedure project that you've been too scared to take on. I hope you no longer feel that panicky overwhelm when you think of everything that has to be documented for your organization, and that *you* have to do it all. Feel instead the relief of opening up a procedure to find step-by-step instructions on how to perform a task that someone else normally does. Experience the effortless induction of a new employee as you show them where to find the answers to the million questions they have when first starting their job.

Although you may still be facing a sizable task, the approaches, tools and processes I've shared in this book provide you the reassurance and the structure that you can undertake any size policy and procedure project in a strategic and systematic way. Do it right and reap the rewards.

Start by cultivating your motivation. Be clear why you are developing your policies and procedures, how they can help you personally in your role, and how they can assist the wider organization you are working in. Once you've accepted that they're actually a good idea and can be extremely useful creating consistency and also supporting yourself and others in the organization, then get down to writing them.

"I'm actually quite excited for you. There is nothing like the comfort of knowing you have a robust set of policies and procedures to support you and your team to produce their best work."

When you start writing, make sure they are:

* as simple as possible

* as short as possible

* as usable as possible

* as current as possible

* written always with the person who will *use* them in mind

* effectively implemented and embedded in the organization

You've got this!

Kirsten Brumby

ACKNOWLEDGMENTS

I acknowledge the wonderful work of the many, many Not for Profit organizations I have worked with and been involved with in varying capacities throughout the years. It has been the need to allow you to focus on your 'core business' and do what it is you do, and help the people you help, that started the process of developing policies and procedures. Our communities would not function if it were not for you, and your organizations don't function without policies and procedures.

Also, to my publisher, Maggie Wilde and all of the team at Mind Potential Publishing, who read and worked with what didn't turn out after all to be the most boring book in the world. Thank you for your perseverance and expert guidance.

MEET THE AUTHOR

KIRSTEN BRUMBY

Kirsten Brumby brings a simple, structured and comprehensive approach to developing policies and procedures. Her unique systems and strategies in the area are sought after by managers and organizations… trying to *keep themselves out of trouble.*

After co-founding a consulting firm that generated 7-figures annually, Kirsten has spent over 20 years Coaching, Training and Consulting for individuals, teams and organizations. She specializes in helping people and organizations find clarity, set outcomes and achieve them.

Kirsten thrives on challenges that others walk away from. She has facilitated initiatives in leadership, small business, not for profit boards, career and life coaching; and has worked internationally across industries including corporate, government and not for profits.

Books by Kirsten Brumby

How to Write Effective Policies and Procedures

The System that Makes the Process of Developing Policies and Procedures Easy

This book is a step-by-step guide to do-it-yourself policies and procedures from the self-confessed policies and procedures pragmatist. Kirsten has nailed the task that many of us dread and now shares her secrets.

NOW WHAT?

A Step-By-Step Approach to Land Your New Job or Career

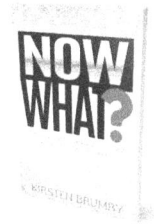

When embarking on a new career or applying for a new job it is extremely hard to stand out from the crowd.

This book provides clarity about that next step. Kirsten guides you to: explore what you *really* want, whether that's to leave your current job, or start a new career. Learn the steps to find clarity and make a decision. Make your resume stand out from the crowd. How to write cover letters and selection criteria responses that make your application irresistible and then shine at that interview.

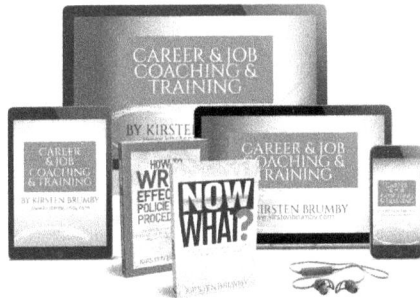

Online Programs By Kirsten Brumby

▶ How to Get your Job Application Noticed and Secure that Job Interview

▶ How to be Outstanding in Interviews and Land that Job

▶ How to Get Clarity About Your Next Career Move

W: www.kirstenbrumby.com | E: contact@kirstenbrumby.com

To download free resources from the author go to
www.howtopoliciesandprocedures.com/resources

www.ingramcontent.com/pod-product-compliance
Lightning Source LLC
Chambersburg PA
CBHW060239030426
42335CB00014B/1533